short-term missions
WORKBOOK

FROM MISSION TOURISTS TO GLOBAL CITIZENS

TIM DEARBORN

IVP Books

An imprint of InterVarsity Press
Downers Grove, Illinois

InterVarsity Press
P.O. Box 1400, Downers Grove, IL 60515-1426
World Wide Web: www.ivpress.com
E-mail: email@ivpress.com

InterVarsity Press® is the book-publishing division of InterVarsity Christian Fellowship/USA®, a student movement active on campus at hundreds of universities, colleges and schools of nursing in the United States of America, and a member movement of the International Fellowship of Evangelical Students. For information about local and regional activities, write Public Relations Dept., InterVarsity Christian Fellowship/USA, 6400 Schroeder Rd., P.O. Box 7895, Madison, WI 53707-7895, or visit the IVCF website at <www.intervarsity.org>.

Scripture quotations, unless otherwise noted, are from the New Revised Standard Version of the Bible, copyright 1989 by the Division of Christian Education of the National Council of the Churches of Christ in the USA. Used by permission. All rights reserved.

The suggested language acquisition phrases in appendix three are adapted from "First Steps in Language Learning" by Dr. Miriam Adeney and are used by permission.

The cultural research questions in appendix three are taken from A Time for Risking by Miriam Adeney © 1987 and are used by permission.

Permission is granted to reproduce the materials in appendix four for use in churches and missions training.

Cover design: Cindy Kiple

Cover image: Jon Allen/Illustration Works

ISBN 978-0-8308-3233-0

Printed in the United States of America ∞

Library of Congress Cataloging-in-Publication Data

Dearborn, Tim.
   Short-term missions workbook / Tim Dearborn.
     p. cm.
Includes bibliographical references.
   ISBN 0-8308-3233-5 (pbk.: alk. paper)
   1. Short-term missions. I. Title.
   BV2063.D42 2003
   266—dc21

2003008234

P	28	27	26	25	24	23	21	20	19	18	17	16	15
Y	27	26	25	24	22	21	20	19	18	17	16	15	

To the thousands of non-Western Christian leaders

who receive our Western short-term mission teams

with overwhelming hospitality.

You are our mentors, teachers, guides and fellow pilgrims.

May God continue to bless and encourage you.

CONTENTS

INTRODUCTION

I have gone on more short-term mission trips than I can count—to places such as Haiti, Dominican Republic, Korea, Japan, Thailand, Malaysia, China, India, Nepal, Kuwait, Palestine, Croatia, Romania, Kenya, Cameroon and Tanzania. In addition, our family served overseas for seven years, and my current position at World Vision involves at least one international trip each month. I am grateful for these extraordinary opportunities.

Yet I sometimes ask myself if our mission service reflects my family's commitment to Christ or our desire for adventure? Have we gone in response to God's call or because we live in an affluent society? Maybe it's a combination of these.

The deeper question is how can our engagement in short-term missions bear the fruit for God's kingdom that the investment of resources, made by the body of Christ, in our travels deserves? This is a question I must ask myself every time I travel.

I have seen the transforming power of short-term mission trips. God uses them to change lives—both of the people who go and of those whom they serve. The constant refrain of participants is how much they grew in their relationship with Christ, how much they learned about community and how challenged they were by the commitment and joy of the people they visited. Lives are formed, and vocations are clarified through short-term mission experiences.

However, I've also seen trauma generated by these trips. Some people come back depressed and confused. Some hosts sigh with relief when their short-term visitors depart. Surely this is not what God intends.

Currently the Western church spends as much on short-term mission trips as it does on long-term missionaries. Clearly this has become a dominant dimension in churches' mission involvement.

This book is my attempt to help us discover how to do it right. Our funds and lives must be invested wisely for the kingdom and not merely for spiritual adventurism.

The resources provided in this workbook have been used to prepare hundreds of people in dozens of churches. They've been carefully tested, evaluated, revised and reviewed. They will help individuals and teams make the most of their short-term experience—personally, for those they serve and for the kingdom. They will protect us from being mission tourists and propel us into lives of global citizenship.

WHO SHOULD USE THIS WORKBOOK?

High school, university and adult mission teams have successfully used this workbook. It is also valuable for individuals and families preparing for crosscultural service and for businesspeople who travel abroad. Those involved in sending people across cultures (mission agency staff, church mission committees, college short-term mission program leaders and youth pastors) can use it to gain greater understanding of the issues that short-term mission participants experience. This will enhance their selection and support of team members. While the focus is on mission trips to a culture different than one's own, these certainly don't need to be international. Many of the insights and attitudes explored in this workbook are appropriate for involvement in our own cities.

HOW TO USE THIS WORKBOOK

If you are going as part of a team, plan to meet together for eight sessions in orientation and preparation; then meet two more times several months after you've returned. Suggestions for group leaders to enhance discussion and reflection are provided in the appendixes at the end of the workbook.

It is recommended that participants study the workbook prior to the group sessions and come prepared with responses to the questions. Each chapter in the workbook is divided into three sections, requiring about an hour of work apiece. Chapters also begin with a recommended group activity to help teams grow together. Participants are encouraged to read two supplemental resource books, *Beyond Duty: A Passion for Christ, a Heart for Mission* and

Mack and Leeann's Guide to Short-Term Missions. Specific chapters are recommended as background reading throughout the workbook. This will enhance participants' understanding and preparation, but the workbook can be useful without the additional reading as well.

Bible study is basic to this workbook, for the Bible is a crosscultural mission manual. There are Bible studies incorporated into most chapters. Participants are encouraged to use these for personal devotions each week prior to the group meeting. The emphasis on Bible study will be strongest in the beginning; in fact, you'll note that the chapters get shorter as departure gets closer—knowing that the pace of life picks up before you leave.

OTHER RECOMMENDED ACTIVITIES

- Start a mission-trip journal—one that includes your reflections during preparation, while on the trip and after returning. You may want to paste your personal mission statement, the team covenant and the "Eight Great Questions" that will be explored in this workbook at the front of the journal. These can be a constant point of reference for you during the trip and upon return.

- Develop relationships with people in your hometown who are from a background similar to that of the people you will be visiting. One of God's great gifts to us in multiethnic America is that most of us don't have to wait until we get off an airplane to meet someone from a different ethnic and cultural background.

- Attend a church service of a cultural or language group that is similar to the one you will be visiting.

- Invite people from that background to visit one of your preparation meetings.

- Invite them to your home for dinner as well. They may reciprocate by inviting you to theirs.

- Seek to learn several common phrases in the dominant language of the people among whom you will be living. This gesture of respect will go a long way toward building bridges. Appendix three lists some helpful phrases.

- Learn as much as possible about the place where you are going before you leave. Some key culture and country research questions are also listed in appendix three.

WHAT THIS WORKBOOK WON'T PROVIDE

This workbook doesn't go through the issues of selecting a destination, travel planning, getting immunizations and trip safety. These are well covered by many other excellent resources, several of which are listed in the recommended reading section of appendix two. Of particular note are the following two books: *Sending Out Servants* by Vicki Tanin, Jim Hill and Roy Howard, and *The Essential Guide to the Short Term Mission Trip* by David C. Forward. Rather than addressing how to prepare a *trip*, this workbook focuses on how to prepare *people*—the theological, spiritual, relational and missiological aspects of preparation for and return from short-term service.

ACKNOWLEDGMENTS

Several people have made invaluable contributions to this workbook. Any wisdom and insight expressed in it comes from my wife and fellow pilgrim, Kerry, as we have explored and reflected together about God's mission in the world. Tami Anderson Englehorn, short-term mission program advisor at Seattle Pacific University, provided many of the recommended group activities and simulation exercises. She has developed one of the finest short-term mission programs in the United States. Two faculty members at Seattle Pacific University, Dr. Miriam Adeney and Dr. Roy Barsness, also provided learning activities.

one

THE GOD OF MISSION

Y ou are about to enter into a great, wonderful adventure. You are going to discover more about God, yourself, God's people and your place in God's mission. What a privilege! As you go, remind yourself that this is God's world. We need not approach it with our guard up, for Jesus is Lord and all authority in heaven and earth is given to him. Through the incarnation, God embraced this world in all its sinfulness and corruption. As the body of Christ, empowered by the Spirit, we are free to extend that embrace to others.

The way we view the world often determines the quality of our involvement in it. Do we think of the world as a hostile, threatening and alien place, perhaps a place from which we must be protected? Or is the world our home, a safe and friendly place, encompassed by the reign of God?

In this chapter we will examine our attitude toward the world, our understanding of God's involvement in it and our place as participants in God's mission.

SUGGESTED GROUP ACTIVITIES

- Begin the process of getting to know one another by discussing the following questions in pairs: Where have you traveled in the past (for business, vacation or mission)? What are you most excited about for your trip? Then introduce each other to the group.

- In groups of four, discuss the following questions, and then pray together: About what are you feeling fearful? Why do you believe God is calling you to go on this trip?

- Play the "Insiders-Outsiders" simulation game (thirty minutes, see the leader's guide for this chapter in appendix one).

SECTION ONE:
IT'S GOD'S WORLD AND GOD'S MISSION

In the midst of a world and a church that are shaken by crises and controversies, the gospel proclaims that "we are receiving a kingdom which cannot be shaken" (Heb 12:28) and a hope which is "a sure and steadfast anchor of the soul . . . that enters the inner shrine behind the curtain, where Jesus, a forerunner on our behalf, has entered" (Heb 6:19-20).

To engage in mission is to participate in the coming of the kingdom of God.

- We are to seek first the kingdom of God (Mt 6:33).
- We are to hunger for the justice of the kingdom (Mt 5:6).
- The desire for the kingdom to come should be foremost among our prayerful petitions (Mt 6:10).
- Jesus' first sermon was about the kingdom at hand (Mk 1:14-15; Lk 4:18).
- Jesus said that the purpose of his teaching was the proclamation of the mystery of the kingdom (Lk 8:10).
- History will not end until the kingdom has been preached to all ethnic groups in the world (Mt 24:14).
- Jesus' final instruction on earth concerned the kingdom (Acts 1:1-8). Following his resurrection and prior to his ascension, the Lord devoted his last opportunity for face-to-face teaching to the kingdom.

QUESTIONS FOR REFLECTION AND DISCUSSION

Read Matthew 6:33.
How would you define the kingdom of God?

What does it mean to seek it?

What is your response to Jesus' statement?

"The church of God does not have a mission in the world. The God of mission has a church in the world!"

Beyond Duty, p. 2

What do you think are some of its implications for your short-term mission service?

God is the Lord of our whole lives and calls all people to full-time service. The implications are clear. When we enter the world, we are not entering alien territory. We may find foes and fiends, but Christ is their only true Lord. "He disarmed the rulers and authorities and made a public example of them, triumphing over them" (Col 2:15). When we march in mission, we are part of a victory procession. We move out to claim territory for its king. There is nothing pathetic or besieged about the church in mission. She knows who is Lord and who has won the triumph.

One cannot follow Jesus simply by adding allegiance to him on top of other commitments. Everything is transformed by faith in

Christ: finances and family, ambition and attitudes, priorities and politics. As followers of Christ

- we renounce all other loyalties.
- we worship God with our bodies.
- we have no life apart from the life of God.

Faith in Christ is not merely a way of getting away from the problems of life or finding peace and strength in their midst. Rather, living in Christ radically changes life. All of God's people are engaged in full-time Christian service! As the following Scripture passages indicate, Jesus is very precise about where we are to serve.

QUESTIONS FOR REFLECTION AND DISCUSSION

Read Acts 1:1-10.
What are the four spheres of witness that Jesus describes?

What are the equivalents of each of these four spheres for you?

In which sphere is it easiest/hardest for you to live as a witness?

What does Jesus say is needed before we can be witnesses?

In what ways would you like to more fully receive the power of the Spirit to strengthen your life as a witness?

Sadly, the church has often interpreted this command as something to be completed sequentially. First we take care of our needs at home, then we move out toward the ends of the earth. Other churches have responded to the call to the farthest corners of the world and skipped over their Jerusalem, Judea and Samaria. But we are called and empowered by the Spirit to be witnesses in our community (Jerusalem), our country (Judea), among people of differing cultural backgrounds who live around us (Samaria) and to the ends of the earth—simultaneously, not sequentially!

SECTION TWO:
LEARNING—THE WORLD IS OUR CLASSROOM

One reason why the body of Christ invests in short-term mission is because it is an exceptional discipleship and mission-education experience. God is about to send you into a remarkable classroom—the world—with remarkable teachers—God's people and the Holy Spirit. A good short-term mission experience will lead people to reflect on several sets of pivotal and challenging questions. These "Eight Great Questions" will be explored more fully in the final chapter, but it's helpful to begin thinking about them now.

What can I learn about myself? You will have abundant opportunities to see yourself in new ways. Seek to be open as a learner—even about yourself.

What can I learn about God? Our faith is expanded when we can see it through the eyes of people from a different background. Seek to understand why others believe as they do.

What can I learn about the people of God, about the church, about community? While on a short-term mission trip, we often discover that other Christians' forms of community worship and church life are different from our own. Seek to understand what contributes to a vibrant Christian community.

What can I learn about how culture affects the way we live and understand the gospel? Our perceptions are conditioned by our culture and background. That is an inescapable part of life. However, entering into another culture can give us perspective on our own culture and possibly overcome some of the limitations of our understanding. Seek to gain new insights into the gospel that emerge from a different culture.

What can I learn about justice, economics, poverty and politics? To serve in the developing world or in America's inner cities is to encounter poverty, economic disparity, injustice and structural evil. Why do these exist, what is God doing in response, and to what form of engagement is God calling the church? Seek to explore these tough and urgent issues. Why are some poor and others rich? What does God say about this?

What can I learn about discipleship? When we engage in short-term mission, we often have the privilege of encountering people with a radical dedication to Jesus Christ. We go seeking to grow in our faith; we also go seeking to share it. We end up receiving far more than we expected. Seek to gain one new insight into what it means to be a disciple of Christ. Seek to have one new step of faithfulness permanently incorporated into your life.

What can I learn about a globally appropriate lifestyle? In light of what we learn about poverty and international economics, what are some implications not just for society in general but also for our own lifestyles as Christians? Seek to discern one way you can live differently in response to the needs of others around the world.

What can I learn about my own vocation? Finally, what is God seeking to say to you about your own life and work? What insight do you gain into your calling and God's will for your life? For those who are students, what questions do you want to pursue more fully in your courses and degree programs in light of what you've learned and seen? Seek to understand ways you can steward the gifts, talents and time with which God has entrusted you in order to participate more fully in God's purposes in the world.

QUESTIONS FOR REFLECTION AND DISCUSSION

Evaluate each question in the following way. Note first the questions that surprised you—in other words, the ones you didn't anticipate dealing with on the trip (mark !). Did you find any threatening (mark X)? Finally, which questions most intrigued you and did you find yourself eager to pursue (mark ?)?

1. What can I learn about myself?	
2. What can I learn about God?	
3. What can I learn about community and the church?	
4. What can I learn about culture and its impact on faith?	
5. What can I learn about justice and poverty?	
6. What can I learn about discipleship?	
7. What can I learn about my lifestyle?	
8. What can I learn about my vocation?	

SECTION THREE:
SERVING—GO ON A TREASURE HUNT

The fundamental ministry God would have all of us exercise as short-term visitors and servants in another culture is the ministry of affirmation. God is inviting us on a treasure hunt. Our privilege is to be so led by the Spirit of God that we can find treasures in this new context that had been hidden from our eyes previously. Not only were they hidden from us because we've never been there before, they may even have been hidden from the eyes of the people who live there.

Thus, God invites us to lift up before others' eyes the ways God is at work among and through them, and all the strengths and gifts they are bringing to their own community. We don't go to bring treasures. Nor do we go to take them home. Rather, we help discover treasures that are present among the people with whom we serve, and together with them, we praise God for God's great kindness.

QUESTIONS FOR REFLECTION AND DISCUSSION

Read 1 Corinthians 2:1-5.
What did Paul seek to discover among the people with whom he worked?

What do you think this would mean in your situation?

What might it look like?

What was Paul's appraisal of his own abilities and attitudes in this ministry?

How does this relate to you and your attitudes?

What will it mean, in tangible ways, for you to rely on the Spirit?

Here are some ways we can engage in this treasure hunt.

- *Walk with humility.* Remember, you are showing up late to a meeting. God has been at work among these people long before you arrived!

- *Embrace with affirmation.* Your greatest gift to the people you meet will be affirmation, not criticism.

- *Live with vulnerability.* Don't be afraid of weakness—it's normal.

- *Practice flexibility.* Always expect the unexpected—you're not in control.

- *Live as a student.* Be determined to learn from everyone.

- *Work as a servant.* Be willing to do whatever needs to be done.
- *Speak as a storyteller.* Let the Spirit tell God's story through you.

SECTION FOUR:
TRANSFORMING—KNOW HOW TO RETURN
HOME BY A DIFFERENT ROUTE

The most important aspect of short-term mission service is preparation; the second most important aspect is integration of the experience into the lives of participants once they return home; and the third most important aspect is the trip itself. Obviously, God is going to do wonderful things through you. Otherwise you wouldn't go, and the body of Christ probably wouldn't invest time and money in your service. However, the long-term impact of your service will be deeply affected by the quality of your preparation, and the long-term impact on your own life will be deeply affected by the quality of your debriefing and integration.

Therefore, one gift you can give yourself is to begin preparing now for your return home. Here are some suggestions.

Reflect on the "Eight Great Questions." What might God want you to learn through this short-term mission trip? Keep the questions in mind throughout your trip, and refer to them occasionally.

Find a prayer and debriefing partner who agrees to pray daily for you while you are gone and who is willing to meet with you several times after you return. Seek someone you trust, and give them permission to ask you any question they want. Make commitments before you leave regarding when you will meet.

Pray now for two new relationships God will give you—one with someone on your team and one with a new person you will meet. Commit yourself now to pray for and keep in touch with those two people after you return.

Keep reflecting on the question, How is God calling me to live differently in light of what I experienced?

QUESTION FOR REFLECTION AND DISCUSSION

What's your response to this statement from *Beyond Duty*? "The weakness of much current mission work and much current preaching is that they betray the sense that what is yet to be done is greater than what has already been done" (quoting P. T. Forsyth, *Missions in State and Church* [London: Hodder & Stoughton, 1908], p. 21).

SUGGESTED READING AND LEARNING EXERCISES

Beyond Duty, chapters 1-2
Mack and Leeann's Guide to Short-Term Missions, chapters 2-5

two

LEARNING TO DELIGHT
IN DIFFERENCES

The combination of our sinful prejudices and our cultural, racial, economic and social differences makes us feel alienated from people who are different than us. Actually, according to anthropologist Walter Goldschmidt, "People are more alike than their cultures." We have more in common with other people than whatever it is that separates us, even with people whose way of life is unimaginably different from ours.

In fact, in crossing into another culture, we are going to meet long-lost, distant relatives.

In this chapter we will explore the role of culture in our life and faith—and evaluate our "entry posture," the way we approach life in a new culture.

SUGGESTED GROUP ACTIVITY

The following exercise, the "Church Game," illustrates the impact of culture on our values and perceptions.

- Either individually or as a team, list all the words that come into your mind when you think of the word *church*.

- Now list all the words that you think would come into the mind of a person in the culture you are visiting when they hear the word *church*.

- Examine your lists, and cross out the items that lack a biblical basis.

- Compare your list with the list you wrote for a person in your host culture. What similarities and differences do you notice?

- Compare your reflections with other teams'. What implications and conclusions can you draw from this exercise?

SECTION ONE:
UNDERSTANDING CULTURE

We generally prefer being with people who are like us, and we are threatened by those who are different. Because of this, ethnic cleansing, segregation and culture wars seem to be the order of the day. One of the most urgent needs in our world is for unity that encompasses diversity. This is one of the reasons God sends us in mission: to learn to delight in differences and to demonstrate to the world the quality of community that Paul describes in Galatians 3:28.

Prejudices and preconceptions form the biggest wall we must confront when we seek to cross into another culture. This wall is two-sided. We have prejudices about others, and they have their own about us. Clarifying these stereotypes is crucial to overcoming them. Through exposure to the media, our study of history, the way we were nurtured and personal experience, each of us has developed preconceptions of others. Because of the strong U.S. presence in the world, people from other countries have stereotypes of Americans. Americans also have stereotypes of others.

Table 2.1.

Common stereotypes Americans have of people in the Two-Thirds World	Common stereotypes people in the Two-Thirds World have of Americans
lazy	aggressive
inefficient	preoccupied with tasks
emotional	harshly pragmatic
slow and unmotivated	tense and pressured
rooted in traditions	discontented and lonely
corrupt leaders	corrupt leaders
naïve	educated
strongly interdependent	strongly individualistic
eagerly seeking a better life	securely enjoying the good life
highly spiritual	highly materialistic

QUESTIONS FOR REFLECTION AND DISCUSSION

Evaluate the list of stereotypes in table 2.1. To what extent do you share these impressions of people in the Two-Thirds World and of Americans?

"Since God is wholly Lord, when we encounter his world and his creatures, we are not entering alien territory and facing alien beings."

Which stereotypes would you delete?

What stereotypes would you want to add?

Beyond Duty, p. 30

What challenges and opportunities do these stereotypes create?

One of the keys to overcoming prejudice is to understand the meaning and role of culture in our approach to life. Culture is not merely etiquette and manners. There is no such thing as a person who "ain't got no culture." Everyone is immersed in their culture like a fish is immersed in water. Culture is best defined as an integrated system of learned behavior patterns, social structures, values and beliefs.

Culture is a total way of life, determining in large part what people

- do
- think
- say
- like and dislike
- consider possible and impossible
- believe to be true and false
- regard as acceptable and unacceptable

We learn our own culture unconsciously as children by transmission from one generation to another.

QUESTIONS FOR REFLECTION AND DISCUSSION

What sayings, adages or stories that were frequently told in your family reinforced particular values?

What did you learn from your family regarding the value of work?

play?

success?

education?

family relationships?

friendship?

housekeeping?

conflict resolution?

As you evaluate these values, are any explicitly "Christian"?

Are any contradictory to the Christian faith?

What impact do these values have on your life today?

No culture is simple or primitive. Even cultures with few modern technological devices are highly complex and sophisticated. Surrounding and upholding each culture is a worldview. This forms a culture's understanding of reality. It explains how and why people exist, what their purpose is, what to expect in the future and how to determine what changes are acceptable.

All people share the common impact of culture on their lives.

- To be human is to be part of a culture.

- All cultures are relatively effective at adapting people to their environment and helping them respond to their basic needs.

- Elements of cultures are integrated, so that change in one part affects every other part.

- Every culture thinks its understanding of what is right, good and true is best.

- Cultures are constantly adapting to political, social and natural changes.

- Because cultures are always changing, it is appropriate to compare cultures and to introduce new ideas and ways of doing things. This is how cultures become more effective at helping people cope with the changing realities of life.

SECTION TWO:
STEPPING BETWEEN CULTURES

Curiosity is essential for crosscultural service. When encountering a different culture—and the "strange" ways people act, live and think—our first prayer must be for God to give us curiosity.

We need to have enough curiosity to seek to understand the

meanings behind people's actions, customs and ideas. If we do not penetrate beneath the surface to discover why people do what they do, we will forever be a foreigner, on the outside rather than the inside of people's lives.

In table 2.2, describe what might be the practical, aesthetic, social or hygienic rationale for each custom.

Table 2.2.

Custom	Rationale
Sleep on a platform	
Sleep on the floor	
Wear street shoes in the house	
Take street shoes off in the house	
Eat with silverware	
Eat with hands	

Though the most irritating cultural differences are often petty behavioral ones, the most perplexing are differences in belief. When encountering different beliefs, the first challenge is to understand them—determining the meaning behind them in their particular context—and then to evaluate them according to their consistency with Scripture and the purposes of God.

Use the system below to evaluate the beliefs found in table 2.3.

+   Consistent with the Bible and can be affirmed

−   Inconsistent with the Bible and needs to be transformed

✓   Neutral in regard to the Bible and can be retained

Table 2.3.

Belief	Meaning	Biblical Evaluation + − ✓
Punctuality indicates respect		
Adults should submit to their parents		
Wives should submit to their mothers-in-law		
Efficiency is a high virtue		
Caring for extended family is a primary obligation		
Cleanliness is next to godliness		

QUESTIONS FOR REFLECTION AND DISCUSSION

What criteria did you use to evaluate the beliefs in table 2.3?

Evaluate the following list of biblical customs (adapted from Ralph Covell and Marshall Shelley, "Permanent or Temporary," *Wherever Magazine*, spring 1982, pp. 8-9). Write "U" next to the ones you think are universal, applicable to all people. Write "C" next to the ones that you think are contextually specific.

- Greet one another with a holy kiss (Rom 16:16).
- Be baptized (Acts 2:39).
- Women should pray with their heads covered (1 Cor 11:5).
- Wash one another's feet (Jn 13:14).
- Permit no woman to teach men (1 Tim 2:12).
- Prohibit women from braiding their hair or wearing gold (1 Tim 2:9).
- Long hair on men is a disgrace (1 Cor 11:14).
- Be circumcised (Acts 15:5).
- Lift up your hands when praying (1 Tim 5:9).
- Give to anyone who begs from you (Mt 5:42).
- Owe no person anything (Rom 13:8).
- Show no favoritism to the rich (Jas 2:1-7).

What criteria did you use to determine which were universal and which were contextual?

How would you summarize the principles on which you based your distinction?

SECTION THREE:
ENTERING INTO A NEW CULTURE

Our task in crosscultural communication is to enter into a culture different from our own and to relate the gospel in terms that make sense to the people of that culture. This communication happens when our meanings match their meanings across a bridge of words, lives and actions.

The God we worship takes the initiative and enters into our world, our cultures and our lives. This is the wonder of the incarnation.

QUESTIONS FOR REFLECTION AND DISCUSSION

Read Philippians 2:1-15.
In what ways was Jesus' incarnation a form of crosscultural ministry?

How did he model entering into another culture?

If you have "this attitude in yourselves which was also in Christ Jesus," what will your attitude be toward the world and the people whom you are serving?

How does the following statement from *Beyond Duty* relate to this issue? "We do not go into the world with life as an all too vulnerable possession that must be defended. Rather, we go in the Person who is Life and who has triumphed over all that can possibly attempt to inhibit people from experiencing life's fullness" (p. 37).

How would you like others to pray for you?

Paul describes in Philippians the ways in which God takes the initiative to communicate with us. Our privilege in short-term mission service is to allow the Spirit to guide us as we participate in Christ becoming a part of other people's lives. It is our responsibility to enter into their lives, not to demand that they enter into ours. God has not sent us to judge their lives and values.

In short-term service, our ability to understand and enter into another culture is obviously limited. Therefore, it's all the more important to realize that all cultures are seeking to respond to similar needs. The answers may vary, but people's longings are alike.

Every culture provides varying combinations of answers to six basic issues, listed in table 2.4.

Table 2.4.

Worldview	Responses		
Who are we?	Basically evil	Mixture of good and evil	Basically good
How do we relate to God?	God is totally separate from people	God is different than people, but people can relate to God	People are divine
How do we relate to nature?	People must submit to nature	People must live in harmony with nature	People are to master nature
How do we approach time?	Past-oriented (traditional)	Present-oriented (situational)	Future-oriented (goal-focused)
What is the purpose of human life?	Live in harmony (stress on being)	Grow in virtue (stress on becoming)	Be fruitful (stress on action)
How do we organize our lives as a society?	Authoritarian	Group and community centered	Individualistic

QUESTIONS FOR REFLECTION AND DISCUSSION

How would you evaluate cultural values according to table 2.4?

Indicate with an "M" your own values.

Indicate with an "A" the values of the dominant American culture.

Indicate with a "B" what you think is the biblical value.

Indicate with a "C" what you think is the dominant value of the culture in which you will be serving.

Might Christians from another culture think values other than the ones you marked are biblical?

Which ones, do you think? Why?

What criteria did you use to determine biblical values?

Describe what you think are the keys to effectively entering into another culture, especially for short-term service, and communicating the gospel within it.

In all of this, remember:

- The incarnation shows us that God is the expert at crosscultural communication.
- Creation reminds us that "people are more alike than their cultures."
- Since we are all created in the image of God, we are encountering long-lost, distant relatives in whomever we meet—regardless of how different their lifestyle and situation may be from our own.

SUGGESTED READING AND LEARNING EXERCISES

Beyond Duty, chapter 3
Mack and Leeann's Guide to Short-Term Missions, chapters 6-7
Language acquisition phrases 1-3, appendix three

three

EMBRACING CHANGE

God will never call us into a ministry without providing the abilities we need to participate in God's purposes in it. Cultural differences are opportunities for understanding and communicating the gospel, not merely obstacles or hindrances. We simply need to learn how to use the tools.

In this chapter we will focus on keys to embracing life in a new culture—learning how to overcome our initial shock and cross the bridge of cultural differences into other people's lives.

SUGGESTED GROUP ACTIVITY

Play the "Castaways on a Desert Island" simulation game (see the leader's guide for this chapter in appendix one).

SECTION ONE:
FACING OUR SHARP EDGES

Some have said that adjusting to another culture is as difficult as fitting a square peg into a round hole. People either change to fit into the new culture or they try to change the new culture to be like their own. Otherwise, they will be out of place—squares in their new place. The desire to become more "well-rounded" is a good aspiration but laden with complexities. Often we are surprised at our own reactions when we enter into another culture.

Imagine yourself in the following situations. How do you think you would respond? Rate each one according to the depth of personal trauma you think you might experience, ranging from 1 as easy to 5 as extremely difficult.

You can't communicate because of language differences, and this produces many awkward, embarrassing situations.	1 2 3 4 5
No one seems to understand you or appreciate the sacrifices you've made to come and be with them.	1 2 3 4 5
You can't wear the clothes that feel most comfortable to you because of others' customs.	1 2 3 4 5
The only time you can be alone is at night in bed.	1 2 3 4 5
No one gives you a straight answer. They seem to say yes to everything, even though they may not mean yes and have no intention of doing what you suggest.	1 2 3 4 5
Nothing starts on time. People state a starting time or agree to meet at a certain time, but often things begin an hour later.	1 2 3 4 5
You find yourself craving familiar food. Even a Big Mac™ sounds great.	1 2 3 4 5
Worship services are very emotional, with many people speaking in tongues.	1 2 3 4 5
People stare at you wherever you go, and women and children often beg from you.	1 2 3 4 5
No toilets, no showers, no air conditioning.	1 2 3 4 5

QUESTIONS FOR REFLECTION AND DISCUSSION

Add up your score. How would you rate your flexibility and adaptability?

What other situations might be particularly difficult for you? Why?

Are there things that help you cope with these kinds of situations? What are they?

Chapter 4 of *Beyond Duty* explores the Scriptures that assert Jesus' "spiritual, political, cultural and social authority over all things" (p. 46). How might an understanding of this affect your approach to uncomfortable situations?

SECTION TWO:
FACING THE FACTS OF CULTURE FATIGUE

The secret is out! It's not easy to live in another culture, understand another culture, enjoy another culture and communicate Christ in another culture. Even so, it can still be fun—an amazing adventure in dependency on God and seeing God work in new ways.

Once the tourist stage is over (and this can last anywhere from one hour to several months), we are confronted with differences. If we focus on the difficulties, then our emotions, conversations and correspondence can become filled with thoughts like these.

- *Cultural alienation:* "Life's not the same here."

- *Personal dissonance:* "I don't fit in here. I feel out of place."

- *Activist frustration:* "Nothing works right here."

- *Relational misunderstanding:* "No one seems to care about how I'm doing."
- *Intellectual confusion:* "I'll never figure out how to live here. I'm hopelessly out of place."
- *Emotional tension:* "I don't want to go outside anymore. I'm tired of feeling like a fool."

With these thoughts comes the onslaught of culture shock, or what on short-term trips is better called culture fatigue. After our initial sense of adventure has worn off, we grow tired of coping with newness and differences. We become weary of being on guard, being watched, always seeking to be courteous and having to be cautious lest we do something offensive or, even worse, dangerous. We find ourselves wanting to go home or withdraw. This is not a very pleasant follow-up to the initial eagerness and optimism that propelled us into the new culture in the first place.

Experiencing culture fatigue is not a sign that we shouldn't have come or that we're not "spiritual" enough to cope with crosscultural ministry. Rather, it is a very natural and normal phenomenon caused by falling into the gaps between our home culture and our new one. The key is to find bridges that will carry us over these gaps of cultural differences.

If we don't look for these bridges, we will likely build walls as a way of protecting ourselves. When our basic values are threatened or when we feel thwarted by a new situation, it is natural to do the following.

- *Criticize:* "I look for what's wrong in the new situation and justify my feeling of alienation by attributing the problem to others."
- *Rationalize:* "I never realized I was so patriotic. The way of life in my own country suddenly seems superior to everything in this new place."
- *Withdraw:* "I had no idea how much I enjoyed listening to Christian music on my Discman®. I suddenly find myself craving time alone in my room."

Some of these responses are inevitable. Everyone will experience these feelings and tendencies, but we need not be stuck here. We can choose a different strategy.

QUESTIONS FOR REFLECTION AND DISCUSSION

Choose one of the various reactions described above and imagine yourself in that situation. Taking only two minutes, draw a picture that portrays your feelings.

Paul says in Philippians 4:13, "I can do all things through Christ who strengthens me." Add to your picture something that portrays Christ entering in and giving you strength to respond differently.

SECTION THREE:
CROSSING THE BRIDGE

The God of grace communicates across the divide of our sin. Grace can surmount all the gulfs separating us from others. The bridge is Jesus Christ—God entering into our humanity so that we might participate in God's divinity. The unique advantage Christians have in all crosscultural encounters is that we enter them across the bridge of Jesus Christ. Jesus has gone before us into the lives and cultures we are entering. He carries us there as we participate in his life through the Holy Spirit. This is what Paul means when he refers to us as the "body of Christ" (1 Cor 12).

It is only through Christ that we can fulfill God's call to be instruments of grace in our new culture. Only his grace can help us overcome all the ways we will feel ungracious, critical, lonely, frustrated and angry.

To be instruments of God's grace in crosscultural ministry, we need to build on five dimensions of grace: gratitude, refreshment, acceptance, compassion and expectancy.

Gratitude. When we feel threatened, rejected or thwarted, our natural tendency is to criticize others, complain about our situation and rationalize our behavior.

However, God has not called you into this new culture or into

God takes the initiative in crossing the cultural bridge. You participate in the work of God's Spirit by following him across the cultural bridge and entering into others' lives.

these new relationships to be a critic. Christ did not enter into our world to criticize and complain, but to redeem us and establish his kingdom. Similarly, Christ has not called us into our new culture to criticize and complain about the heat, the dirt, the noise, the inconvenience, the corruption or the loneliness. Complaint and criticism create a bottomless pit, while praise and gratitude are the language of God's kingdom.

Paul calls us to give "thanks to God the Father at all times and for everything in the name of our Lord Jesus Christ" (Eph 5:20). This is essential to traverse the bridge of grace into a new culture. The right to offer suggestions is only gained with time and trust. If you are a short-term visitor, you have not yet gained that right. Therefore, your calling is to find everything you can be thankful for in your new situation with these new people. Your gratitude and affirmation may be your most profound and enduring contribution to their lives.

Refreshment. It will be very difficult to express the resiliency of grace if you are exhausted and not living a balanced life. In order to be gracious with others, we need to first be gracious to ourselves. One aspect of that is seeking healthy refreshment and maintaining a rhythmic life. When we are traveling for a short time, we often "sprint" the entire trip. As a result, we neglect the normal patterns that lead to wholeness.

Table 3.1.

Unhealthy Refreshment	Healthy Refreshment
Escaping behind my personal "mission compound," surrounded by touches of America	Occasional forays into my own culture through meals, films, music and nights in "comfortable" surroundings
Only socializing with other Americans or expatriates	Occasional visits with other Americans
Filling my life with busyness	Taking a day off each week; maintaining regular Bible study and prayer; getting regular exercise and sleep
Fantasizing about life back home	Discovering what people do in my new context to relax and play

QUESTIONS FOR REFLECTION AND DISCUSSION

Complete the following two statements, then answer the questions below.

I feel most relaxed when:

The things I most enjoy doing for refreshment are:

Do you think it will be possible to do these things in your new culture?

What problems might there be with these behaviors? What do you think they would mean in your new culture?

What patterns will you commit yourself to in order to maintain a sense of rhythm?

Acceptance. There is a dimension of reality therapy that is required for crosscultural ministry. We are in our new culture, so we might as well accept it. There's no point in constantly fighting it and standing on the outside as a stranger and judge. Christ accepts us, and he has sent us to manifest his acceptance of others.

Three factors enhance our ability to become people of acceptance.

1. *Friendship.* Seek to develop a friendship with one person within your new culture. Hopefully, this person will be regarded by others in the culture as someone with insight and credibility. Invite this person to be your guide, advocate and teacher. Obviously it is important to prayerfully select the right person. Often the best candidates are the busiest, while the most available may be the worst interpreters of their own culture.

    Remember to be very cautious about stereotypes and generalizations regarding life in that culture. Be cautious also about letting expatriates be your prime guides, for you will likely pick up their prejudices and preconceptions.

2. *Forgiveness.* It is easy to forget the central importance of practicing forgiveness. Forgive yourself for your mistakes, cultural faux pas and negative attitudes; forgive your host culture and the people in it as well. Do not allow yourself to build up resentment.

3. *Finding delights.* Seek to discover what delights God about the people you are serving. He created them, redeemed them and loves them. They are bearers of God's image; therefore, much in their lives will reflect God's character and creativity.

Compassion. Grace flows from compassion, and compassion literally means "to suffer with." The prerequisite for compassion is the willingness to enter into others' lives and share their concerns. We need to continually remind ourselves that we are the ones who've entered other people's culture and home. We are their guests. Therefore, it is our task to adapt and adjust to them, rather than expecting them to adapt and adjust to us.

Compassion is ultimately a gift from God. It grows as we focus on Jesus Christ and as the Spirit of God pours out the love of Christ in our hearts (see Rom 5). The Missionaries of Charity, an order founded by Mother Teresa, pray daily: "Dearest Lord, . . . though you hide yourself behind the unattractive disguise of the irritable, the exacting and the unreasonable, may I still recognize you and say: 'Jesus, . . . how sweet it is to serve you'" (Mother Teresa, *In the Silence of the Heart* [London: SPCK, 1983], p. 41).

Expectations. Disciplining our expectations is a final bridge builder. Guilt, busyness and disappointment are common characteristics of people entering new cultures. Guilt emerges because we don't feel like we are doing enough or accomplishing enough. People have sent us here, and we've come with some sacrifice, hoping to accomplish something. These feelings spill over into busyness. *If only I do more, then maybe I'll succeed. If I appear busy, at least, then others can't criticize me.* This kind of busyness then leads to disappointment. *The experience just isn't measuring up to what I'd hoped it would be.*

To deal with this, we must clarify why we are going on a short-term mission trip. Through this, we can identify some realistic goals and expectations.

QUESTIONS FOR REFLECTION AND DISCUSSION

As you pray about your short-term mission trip, what further insight is God giving you about why he wants you to go?

Write two or three things you believe God wants to accomplish in and through you.

Here are some possible objectives God frequently has for people on short-term mission trips:

- to pray more specifically for people in this new context than you could have if you hadn't gone

- to develop two significant relationships

- to explore a new situation and learn more about God, yourself, people and life

- to affirm people in this new context, demonstrating God's love and compassion

Our experience in another culture will be greatly enhanced as we maintain perspective. We're not the first to cross the bridge into another culture. The future of the human race doesn't hinge on our actions. Remember the words of Walter Goldschmidt, "People are more alike than their cultures."

A good summary of what helps us to adjust to a new culture includes this common advice:

- *Laugh.* Find the humor in the situation and specialize in laughing at yourself (not others).

- *Listen.* St. Francis had it right. Seek first to understand, rather than to be understood.

- *Learn.* God hasn't sent you into the culture to be its judge.

- *Love.* It's the universal language.

- *Live.* Enter in, enjoy the differences and live as a servant.

SUGGESTED READING AND LEARNING EXERCISES

Beyond Duty, chapter 4

Mack and Leeann's Guide to Short-Term Missions, chapters 8-10

Language acquisition phrases 4-6, appendix three

MAXIMIZING PERSONAL GROWTH

How well you understand and can handle a different culture is less important than how well you understand and can handle yourself. Crosscultural encounters provide abundant opportunities for personal growth. Often we discover things about ourselves that we didn't know—some which thrill us, others which dismay us.

The call of the kingdom is not simply to be true to yourself but to be true to your best self, the self you are in Christ, the self he is transforming you into.

In this chapter we will examine more clearly our expectations, strengths and values in order to explore what we bring to crosscultural service. Normally we might begin our preparation here, but it's more appropriate to examine ourselves in light of all that we've studied up to this point.

SUGGESTED GROUP ACTIVITY

As people enter the room, have each person add their ideas to two separate lists: one of common fears about crosscultural encounters and the other of qualities of a good missionary. Refer to these as you discuss the pertinent sections in this chapter.

SECTION ONE: ASSESSING OUR EXPECTATIONS

The quality of our experience in another culture will largely be determined by our expectations and our reasons for being there. Therefore we must be clear about why we are going.

Our motives are like rudders that steer our emotional ship.

They control our attitude, influence our behavior and determine the tone of our experience. It's essential that we know which direction our rudder is pointing if we are to go in the direction we desire. Our motives are always mixed. However, when faced rather than suppressed, motives can be empowering and, when necessary, transformed.

Look over this list of common motivations for crosscultural service, and check those that apply to you.

- Adventure
- Professional development
- A new challenge, a greater sense of fruitfulness
- Love of travel
- The desire to help others
- A desire to experience something exotic
- A commitment to evangelism
- A commitment to social justice
- The desire to be with other friends who are going
- The desire to separate for a while from current obligations
- The need for a change
- The desire to grow in my relationship with God and to depend on God more
- The desire to gain new insight into world need and how others live
- The hope that a new setting will resolve a pressing personal problem
- To seek a new purpose for life
- To explore the possibility of long-term mission service

It's appropriate to expect positive outcomes from a crosscultural experience. We wouldn't do it if we didn't expect good to come from it. In fact, the goal of our preparation is to enable us to have an expectant, affirming approach to life in another culture rather than a fearful, defensive one. It is also to clarify our expectations so that they can be realistic and fruitful.

Our fears are another dimension of our expectations. Unrecognized, they can control us. When faced and shared with others,

they can lose their power over us. The following is a list of common fears people face in other cultures. Check those that seem to apply to you.

- Physical harm or illness
- Embarrassment
- Loneliness
- Looking foolish, making mistakes
- Failure
- Dying
- Depression and discouragement
- Conflict with teammates
- Financial difficulties
- Losing my place among friends back home
- Not being able to fit back into life at home when I return

QUESTIONS FOR REFLECTION AND DISCUSSION

In what type of situations do you tend to become anxious?

What are some of your biggest fears about this trip?

What do you think will help you overcome your fears?

How can your teammates best assist you?

Describe in a few sentences why you believe God wants you to go on this trip. Shape this into a personal mission statement to guide your preparation, your trip and your return. (Refer back to your answer on page 45.)

How has your understanding changed as you've engaged in this preparation?

What do you hope will be the impact of this experience on you?

On your place of service?

SECTION TWO:
ASSESSING OUR STRENGTHS

We each bring gifts and abilities to our team and our new culture. God has not created us merely as an assortment of expectations and fears. We are also unique expressions of God's creativity and kindness. God has gifted each person and empowered them by the Holy Spirit so that God's love might be expressed through them. In Romans 12:3 Paul calls us to "have a sane estimate of your own capabilities." This implies being able to recognize and accept strengths that God has given you. Often it is easier for us to admit our fears and weaknesses than our strengths.

Evaluate yourself on a scale of 1 to 5, with 1 being low and 5 high, according to the following list of qualifications that national church leaders most frequently desire in missionaries.

Qualities of a Good Missionary

Loves Christ	1	2	3	4	5
Loves people	1	2	3	4	5
Wants to become friends with people in the host culture	1	2	3	4	5
Willing to serve alongside others and, together, discover God's will	1	2	3	4	5
Flexible and doesn't always insist on her own way	1	2	3	4	5
Willing to learn how God's strength is perfected in weakness	1	2	3	4	5
Able to laugh at himself	1	2	3	4	5
Desires to work as part of a team	1	2	3	4	5

QUESTIONS FOR REFLECTION AND DISCUSSION

In which area do you think you are strongest?

In which area do you most need to grow?

In addition to this list of missionary qualities, what are three other abilities and strengths that you believe God has given you?

For what would you like others to pray for you?

SECTION THREE:
ASSESSING OUR VALUES

We not only take our expectations, fears and strengths, we also take our values into crosscultural service. This baggage, which requires no packing, is often the heaviest to carry. The following table compares some common Western values with the gospel.

Table 4.1.

Common Western Values	Gospel
Do not trust anyone but yourself.	Trust God, God's Word and God's people (Heb 6:18-19; 2 Tim 3:16).
Do your own thing; please yourself.	Let God work out God's will through you (Eph 2:2-10).
Only the present is important.	The past, present and future are valued (Rom 1:4; Jer 29:11-14).
Question all authorities; all values are relative.	Authorities and absolutes are real and essential (Rom 13; Eph 6).
Freedom requires the elimination of restrictions.	Freedom requires submission to God (Gal 5).
Greatness is found through climbing to success.	Greatness is found through descending as a servant (Mk 10:42-45; Jn 12:1-17).
You are ultimately alone.	You belong to God and to God's family (1 Cor 12:13-27).
You are the product of your circumstances.	You are created by God, and change is possible and essential (2 Cor 5:17; Eph 4:20-24).

The following is a list of common American idioms.

- Do your own thing.
- Mind your own business.
- Respect others' privacy.
- Do the best you can.
- If it feels good, then do it.
- Where there's a will, there's a way.
- You can do anything you set your mind to.
- Cleanliness is next to godliness.
- Clean your plate.

QUESTIONS FOR REFLECTION AND DISCUSSION

Which of these values and idioms are common to you?

"A good missionary is someone who loves Jesus and loves Haitians."

Haitian pastor, in
Beyond Duty

Are there others that reflect the values on which you've been nurtured?

Chapter five of *Beyond Duty* reflects on the utter sufficiency of Christ over our struggles and suffering: "Our life in mission resembles reading the history of an ancient battle. We know how it will end. We know that one day, lions and lambs will frolic together, all tears will be wiped away, all sorrows will cease and all

suffering will end. We know that all injustices will be righted, and injuries healed, that every knee will bow in adoration of the Lamb who was slain. God will dwell among his people. Further, we know that one day we personally will be clothed with the right-eousness and dignity of our Lord Jesus, and will dwell in the per-manent home he's prepared for us" (p. 59). What is your response to this statement?

Return to the "Eight Great Questions" mentioned in chapter two of this workbook. Which ones are looming larger in your life—areas which you are now more eager to explore?

How do you hope your experience will help you to explore these questions more fully?

Evaluate the personal mission statement you've written describing why you are going on this trip. Are there revisions you would like to make to it? Write or rewrite your personal mission statement.

SUGGESTED READING AND LEARNING EXERCISES

Beyond Duty, chapter 5
Mack and Leeann's Guide to Short-Term Missions, chapter 11
Language acquisition phrases 7-8, appendix three
Take a short personality test (a modified Myers-Briggs) such as the one available online at <www.humanmetrics.com>.

WORKING TOGETHER AS A TEAM

The love we have for one another as Christians is the best proof of the truth of the gospel. Learning to work together as a team with our coworkers and people from our new culture is essential for an effective witness. The gospel is best communicated by the body of Christ—not by isolated individuals.

In this chapter we will examine some keys to effective relationships on our own team, and how to expand our team to incorporate people from our new context.

SUGGESTED GROUP ACTIVITIES

- Play the "Human Knot" game. Have six to ten people line up and hold hands (this could be done according to teams). While the last person stands in place, the first person should pull the line, weaving in and out of the line members (without anyone letting go) until they've created a giant human knot. Without speaking or letting go, they then should try to disentangle themselves.

- Play "Blindfolded Birthdays." Blindfold each member of the same group and give them the task of lining up according to height. Then tell them they must reorganize themselves into a new line according to birthdays, this time without speaking.

- Debrief the two games by discussing these questions. How did your team figure out this game? What kind of role did you end up playing for the team? Did you notice anyone taking on a leadership position? Who? Did you notice others playing other roles? What roles and who? What might this tell you about your group and what to expect in your time together on the trip?

- Create a team covenant. At the end of this chapter are some questions for writing a team covenant. This process may take several weeks, so begin simply by brainstorming, with one person taking notes. Then have two people on each team volunteer to take the ideas and draft a team statement by the next week. Have another volunteer a Scripture verse that could be your team's theme verse.

SECTION ONE:
THE CHALLENGES OF WORKING TOGETHER

Relationships are the biggest source of joy, as well as of frustration, discouragement and a sense of failure in crosscultural ministry. We go to build relationships with people who are different than we are. That is not easy to do. Surprisingly, however, the biggest relational problems crosscultural workers have are with their coworkers.

Suddenly we are thrust together with people we probably did not choose as our neighbors, friends, coworkers, counselors and even support group. No wonder tensions arise! Add to this the challenges of adjusting to a new language and culture, fatigue and jet lag, loneliness, homesickness, physical discomfort and spiritual conflict. Even excellent relationships are placed under severe stress.

Jesus said, "All people will know that you are my disciples by the love you have for one another" (Jn 13:35). Good teams don't just happen. They are built, and building a team takes time—time that is best begun before you leave.

Gandhi was once asked, "What will it take for India to become Christian?" He replied, "All that is necessary is for the Christians to be Christian." How can we build relationships with our team of coworkers that will become an effective witness for the gospel?

QUESTIONS FOR REFLECTION AND DISCUSSION

List things that might jeopardize your effectiveness as a team.

Gandhi was once asked, "What will it take for India to become Christian?" He replied, "All that is necessary is for the Christians to be Christian."

In *Beyond Duty*, this comment is made about Colossians 3:12-13: "Paul exhorts us to bear with one another in compassion, kindness, humility, gentleness and patience. Yet many of us in mission actually alienate people wherever we go. People inadvertently find themselves feeling inadequate, uncommitted, and unspiritual. They ask themselves, 'Why am I not more . . . ?'" (p. 67). What are some of your reactions to this?

How does the quote from *Beyond Duty* apply to your relationships with the other team you will be joining—the team of people from your host context?

KEYS TO EFFECTIVE TEAMWORK

Rely on Christ. Christ is alive in you and in your coworkers, even though they may act differently and believe differently than you. Dietrich Bonhoeffer reminds us in *Life Together* that we dare not relate directly to one another. We must allow Christ to be our intermediary—the bridge between us as we relate to one another through him.

We rely on Christ in our relationships with our coworkers by

- praying regularly for and with our coworkers
- seeking God's transformation of ourselves, not just our coworkers

- seeking to view others as Christ views them
- affirming what is praiseworthy in others

Respect others. It's so obvious that it seems pedantic to repeat. However, whenever I allow my mouth to speak words that disrespect others (even when they are not present), I build a wall.

- Pray regularly that God will deepen your respect for your coworkers.
- Avoid sharing frustrations about one coworker with another. Let God be the receptacle of your expressions of frustration.
- Don't write lists of grievances about others.
- Let others succeed.

QUESTIONS FOR REFLECTION AND DISCUSSION

What teams have you been a part of in the past? What made them positive or negative experiences?

What's the most helpful role you feel you can exercise on a team?

What should members of your team know about you in order to enhance their work with you?

How can you keep your team from becoming a clique?

How can you best respond as a team to romance between unmarried team members?

What goals do you have for your personal contribution to your team?

SECTION TWO:
EXPANDING THE TEAM

God has not sent you into another culture simply to build wonderful relationships with your coworkers from home. God has sent you to build friendships with people in your new context. One of the most powerful expressions of the truth of the gospel is that people from radically different contexts can love each other.

According to the Mennonite Central Committee, "The primary relationship of each worker on the field is with the local fellowship of believers. As much as possible, the overseas workers should enter fully into the life and work of the local church in the area where he is assigned, thus giving visible expression to the unity of believers and the universality of the church."

Here are some ways we can expand our team to include people from our host culture.

Seek their friendship. We will never become one of "them" if all our fellowship is with "us." The us-them distinction needs to be surmounted by the Holy Spirit. This can only happen when we merge our fellowship with theirs, seeking support, worship and encouragement with them. We will have time to focus on our relationships with our teammates from home once we return. Until then, it's time to expand the team and build new relationships.

Share ourselves with them. We must not allow ourselves to become the stereotypical Americans who seem to have it all together. We need to let people know our hopes and fears, doubts and inadequacies. Surprisingly, this will build their respect for us and their confidence in God. If you, feeling as inadequate as you do, can enable wonderful ministry and compassionate caring, then they will be encouraged to trust that God can do the same through them. God's strength is indeed made perfect in our weakness. If we never admit our own inadequacies (some of which are all too visible for everyone to see), we only deepen their sense of dependency and worthlessness.

Submit to their decisions. Even when we disagree or think our way is better, we need to honor and submit to their decisions. That is not easy, but we are their guests! We must seek to learn the reasons behind their decisions. Once we understand, perhaps then we can determine if a different course of action might be preferable in the future.

We need to choose the long view, allowing ourselves to lose a few battles so that the war might be won.

Serve according to their cultural pattern. One of the hardest dimensions of crosscultural service is learning to do things their way instead of demanding that they do them ours. For example, in many places of the world, saying no to a request is intolerably rude. Therefore, people may say yes but never do what you think they've agreed to. Or they may ask you to come back later, and only after several return visits do you realize that they really were saying no.

QUESTIONS FOR REFLECTION AND DISCUSSION

Which of these four dimensions of teamwork do you find most challenging? Why?

Read Christ's prayer for his followers in John 17. What is his desire for our relationships?

Through this prayer, Jesus shows us ways in which we can experience unity. What specific insights does he give?

What are some of the biggest challenges you think you will face in your new, expanded team?

Consider this statement from *Beyond Duty:* "Because the kingdom of God is a web of relationships, and because relationships are inherently bilateral, mutual and reciprocal, we are free to be partners in mission with the global church. . . . The word 'partner' comes from *parcener*, which means 'co-heir.' To be partners with someone is to be co-heirs of the future. That is precisely who we are in the Body of Christ—co-heirs of all God's promises" (p. 68). What does this statement imply for your incorporation of people from your new context into your team?

What can you do to keep the diversity of your team from degenerating into division, both with your coworkers from home and your new, expanded team?

SECTION THREE:
MINISTERING AS A TEAM

Ministering to our host country. As a team, you have the privilege of ministering to the country that you are visiting. You are their guests. As guests, the normal keys to civility prevail:

- courtesy
- respect for others' customs
- graciousness regarding inconveniences
- patience when things are done differently

Exercising caution regarding criticism. Be exceedingly cautious about voicing criticisms of your host country's government, economic or social policies, living standards, customs, or religious beliefs. Even in letters back home and in conversations with co-workers and missionaries, exercise restraint and discretion. We are guests, and to speak critically would be like criticizing the home and meal of someone who has hosted you for dinner. God has not sent us to be critics.

Praying about complaints. When confronted with things we dislike or disagree with, we should deal with them in prayer. Ask others to help you understand why things are as they are, rather than indicating that you think they shouldn't be that way. At times, God may have us speak out and instigate change, but that can only be done once we have earned credibility. Part of this credibility will depend on people knowing that we like them and their country. It does no one any good to continually compare our host country to "back home"—it diminishes our contentment, and it diminishes the confidence of the people with whom we are working.

Dumping garbage in a journal. We have to express our frustrations somewhere. Our journal is the best place. It's objective and it's confidential. Occasionally we may also need to talk with a co-worker, but that should be done with great caution, lest we drag others down and build walls between us and our hosts. Let the Holy Spirit be your comforter instead. After all, that is one of the Spirit's jobs—and specialties! Let your frustrations become an opportunity for encountering new depths of intimacy with the Spirit of God.

Remembering whom we represent. Though the brief paragraphs above have been filled with "shoulds," they are pivotally important in our role as ambassadors for Christ. Ultimately, in the eyes of our hosts, we are not merely representing ourselves, our opinions and our home country. We are representing Christ.

Ministering to our home country. One of the most important ministries we have is to our friends and supporters back home. They have sent us to be their eyes, ears, hands and heart. We represent them. We learn for them and thus have wonderful opportunities to minister to them. Our correspondence with them will make them feel like a central part of our team.

In everything we write and say to people back home, a cardinal rule is to assume that someone from our host country is reading or hearing what we are saying.

- Would they feel respected, honored and affirmed by what we write?
- Would they agree with it?
- Would they regard our words as a fair representation of their life, culture and country?

QUESTIONS FOR REFLECTION AND DISCUSSION

It's time to draft a team covenant. Write a brief statement that each of you can keep in the front of your trip journal, conveying the commitments you are making to one another regarding

the qualities you want to characterize your relationships

how you will spend your time together

team worship and prayer

how you will make financial and logistical decisions

how you will incorporate others from your new context into your lives and relationships

how you will deal with difficulties and tensions that may arise

After you have written your ideas above, discuss them with your team and agree on a common statement.

SUGGESTED READING AND LEARNING EXERCISES

Beyond Duty, chapter 6
Mack and Leeann's Guide to Short-Term Missions, chapters 14-15
Language acquisition phrases 9-10, appendix three

COMMUNICATING CLEARLY

Relax! The Holy Spirit is already at work in the hearts and lives of the people with whom you will be working. We don't begin God's work. Rather, we enter into an ongoing conversation that God has already been having with people. Our privilege is to discover what God is doing and to participate in it, enabling others to see Christ more fully. We are not solo communicators of the gospel. The Spirit of God speaks through us. Furthermore, in the midst of any linguistic obstacles that might impair our communication, love is the universal language.

In this chapter we will explore some simple keys to effective crosscultural communication of the gospel. It need not be as hard as we make it seem!

SUGGESTED GROUP ACTIVITY

In small groups, participate in the following "Bombs and Bridges" exercise.

- Have each person select a bomb and a bridge from the following list without telling anyone else.

Bombs	Bridges
Forget names	Use names
Avoid eye contact	Maintain eye contact
Glance around room	Focus on the people in your group
Interrupt	Wait until others are done
Question others' facts	Affirm others' ideas
Overreact	Maintain decorum
Overprotect—treat others as childish	Affirm others' worth and independence

- Then converse with each other for five minutes about the past week, with each person trying to use their bomb and their bridge during the conversation.

- Change the topic, and for five minutes, imagine you are trying to make a decision as a group about where to eat. Each of you has a different desire. Be sure to use your bomb and bridge again.

- Discuss the experience, guessing the bridges and bombs used by others. Then, as a group, summarize the keys to effective listening.

SECTION ONE:
FOCUS ON CHRIST

We are not seeking to import Christianity into our new culture. We are not seeking to communicate a set of doctrines and dogmas. We are not seeking to make people like us. We are not even seeking to make people into Christians like us.

Instead, we are participating in the ongoing activity of the Spirit of God to encourage people as they grow in Christ.

This involves standing back and watching to see what unique form others' relationship with Christ takes. Communication is not a matter of clever strategies, manipulative methods or practiced speeches. Rather, it is one friend telling another friend about his Best Friend.

In order to communicate Christ with clarity and conviction, we must know him and be satisfied with him. If we have not found him to be the way, truth and life for ourselves, we certainly will not be able to persuade others that he is that for them.

Leslie Wetherhead, a British preacher, once said, "My friends, may I warn you from my own failures, that while you will be of immense help to the cause of Christ by being able to defend its intellectual position, you will be a thousand times more potent missionary if you exhibit a life that Christ has changed, if you show in your nature those fruits for which all people hunger, if you love the quiet serenity, that endless good will, that deep joy, and that passionate purpose which are among the important marks of a nature surrendered to our Lord."

If Christ has changed our lives, then why are we often hesitant and awkward when it comes to evangelism? In *Out of the Salt-*

shaker, author Becky Pippert writes, "The way we communicate is as important as what we communicate. In fact, the two cannot really be separated. Our attitude and style communicate content just as do our words. If we notice that non-Christians seem embarrassed, apologetic or defensive, it is probably because they are picking up our attitude. If we assume they will be absolutely fascinated to discover the true nature of the gospel, they probably will. If we project enthusiasm, not defensiveness, and if we carefully listen instead of sound like a recording . . . non-Christians will become intrigued" (p. 128).

What a striking thought! How often have I approached someone assuming that they would be absolutely fascinated to hear about Christ? Pippert suggests the following strategies for overcoming any hesitancy we might feel.

Expose but don't impose. We do not try to convert people. That is the work of the Holy Spirit. Our role is not to force faith on others or to convince them of the errors in their beliefs and behaviors. Our role is to reveal Christ to them and invite them to consider faith in him.

Take it easy. Casual, relaxed references to Christ as a part of normal conversation are much more effective than anxiously plotting out how to "get a good word in about Jesus." We can talk about Jesus with the same freedom among non-Christians as among Christians.

Eliminate "God-talk." We need to find ways to communicate Christ in fresh, creative ways without Christian clichés or jargon.

Ask good questions. You don't need to have all the answers. Nor are you the defender of the truth of the gospel. God can defend God. Through questions, encourage others to explore what they believe about Christ.

QUESTIONS FOR REFLECTION AND DISCUSSION

How has your life changed since you became a Christian?

More recently, what impact has Christ had on your life?

How would your parents, spouse or best friend describe the impact of Christ on your life?

Do you think it is necessary for all people to believe in Christ? Why or why not?

When was the last time you talked with someone who was not a Christian about Jesus Christ?

Why is it that we often feel awkward about sharing Christ with people who are not Christians?

What can help us overcome that?

SECTION TWO:
THE MEETING OF MEANINGS

In our encounters with people, we are not only concerned with putting the Word into our words. We also want to put the Word into our hearers' words. Only then will what we mean to say be what they hear us say.

God calls us not only to be aware of the message and our conduct as the messenger but also of the one receiving the message. The responsibility for clear communication rests with the messenger, not with the person receiving the message.

QUESTIONS FOR REFLECTION AND DISCUSSION

Discuss the communication gap between the following sender and receptor in table 6.1.

Table 6.1.

Sender	Receptor
Since I was saved I've lived a victorious life.	He suddenly became thrifty and now wins all his conflicts.
I have constant peace.	Nothing bothers her?
God told me . . .	He's hearing voices?
I'm really getting into the Word.	Where is that?
I love our worship services—they're filled with passion.	Hmm. What kind of loose place is this?

Can you think of other clichés that Christians tend to use?

Pick several of your favorite phrases, and try to assess what they might mean to someone who has never heard them.

"Communica-

tion happens

when my

meanings

meet your

meanings

across a

bridge of

words, and

they match."

David Augsburger,

Communicating

Good News

How could you communicate the same meaning without using a specialized vocabulary?

Write your testimony in your own words, as you might normally tell it. Limit it to two paragraphs.

Circle all the words you used that might seem strange or confusing to someone not familiar with your specialized vocabulary (including the word *testimony* itself).

Rewrite it using words or images that you think would be more familiar to someone who has had no contact with Christians.

Evaluate each person's testimony in the following ways.

Is it specific?

Is it relevant to the hearers?

Is it winsome?

Is it fresh and clear?

SECTION THREE: FOCUS ON PEOPLE

Sometimes we are so focused on getting the message and our conduct as the messenger right that we lose sight of the people with whom we are communicating.

For communication to be effective, it must relate to the real-life situation of the people with whom we are communicating. Less important than what is on our mind as the messenger is what is going on inside the minds and lives of the receptors.

There are three common principles for effective communication (see table 6.2). As you review them, reflect on ways you see them reflected in Jesus' communication with people.

Table 6.2.

Communication Principle	Implications	Expression in Jesus' Life
1. Be listener-centered	Know the people with whom you are speaking. What are their interests? How would they describe their primary needs? How is the Spirit at work in their lives? To what extent do they trust you? What is the risk or potential cost to them if they receive Christ?	
2. Take the initiative	God did not wait for us to come to him. He took the initiative. Jesus says, "As the Father has sent me, so do I send you." We too should take the initiative.	
3. Move into their world	Rather than forcing others to understand us, our responsibility is to be understandable to them. We do this by • being life specific—using illustrations that are appropriate for their context • leading them to discovery—allowing them to develop their own answers • minimizing distance—sharing the same needs they have	

What to say when you're invited to speak in church. Due to hospitality and a desire to learn from God, people often invite visitors to speak in church. Sometimes pastors will dispense with their prepared sermon to offer overseas visitors the pulpit. In these situations it is important to be prepared to give words of greeting and testimony. However, it is often acceptable and honoring of the people there if you keep this brief. You can explain that you have come to learn from them and ask the pastor to please go ahead with the sermon he or she has prepared. If you are unsure what to do, ask your host.

Life message presentation. In order to be prepared, it is well worth preparing words of greeting and a brief testimony now. Dr. Roy Barsness offers the following helpful guide for giving a testimony.

- Pray for wisdom.

- Write out your presentation.

- Relate one current situation in your life, being honest and not exaggerating (make sure it's a situation people there will understand, considering lifestyle and life-situation differences). Give enough details to arouse interest, but leave some unknowns.

- Include one, but not more than two, Scripture verses.

- Remember we are signs pointing to Jesus, not to our success, our church, our school or our country.

- Keep it short—no more than three minutes.

- Do not use Christian jargon (such as *saved, conviction* or *sanctified*).

- People want to hear how Christ makes a difference in life now.

- Memorize your life message so you can deliver it naturally and with confidence.

- Speak loudly, clearly and concisely, in a natural and relaxed tone of voice. Avoid assuming a "ministerial twang."

- Avoid mannerisms such as rubbing your nose, jingling coins in your pocket, saying "uh" or swaying.

- Look at your audience; do not stare at the ground or look only at one person.

- Smile. Be enthusiastic in your sharing.

QUESTIONS FOR REFLECTION AND DISCUSSION

Like Jesus, Paul was a master communicator. Study the following incidents in Paul's life to discover how he adapts his presentation of the gospel to the needs and frame of reference of his listeners.

Read Acts 17:26-32.
Where does Paul begin his ministry in Athens?

How does he build a bridge with the Athenians?

How would you evaluate the results of his Mars Hill sermon?

Read Acts 26:1-30.
How does Paul build a bridge with Agrippa?

What does his message focus on?

How would you evaluate the results of this sermon?

What implications do you draw about communicating the gospel from Paul's two different approaches?

What do you think God needs to overcome in your life to make you a more comfortable, natural and appropriate communicator of the gospel?

How would you like your team to pray for you regarding this?

SUGGESTED READING AND LEARNING EXERCISES

Mack and Leeann's Guide to Short-Term Missions, chapter 13
Language acquisition phrases 11-13, appendix three

STAYING SPIRITUALLY FRESH

Our secularized culture has disarmed us for the spiritual nature of life. We forget that "we wrestle not against flesh and blood, but against principalities, against powers" (Eph 6:12). As a result, we usually rely on our own resources when we encounter adversity, and thus we are quickly discouraged and defeated. To be truly prepared for life, we need to know how to be fed, nourished and equipped with the resourceful life of Christ.

In this chapter we will explore the reality of spiritual conflict and the resources God has given us for standing firm in Christ. We will also study a simple spiritual discipline that can help us remain spiritually vibrant.

SUGGESTED GROUP ACTIVITY

Meditate silently on Galatians 2:20 and the daily prayer of the Missionaries of Charity (see bookmarks in appendix four).

SECTION ONE:
THE NATURE OF THE BATTLE

We may be prepared to dig wells, teach schools, type manuscripts, build buildings, play with kids, program computers, provide medical care and proclaim the gospel, but if we're not prepared for spiritual battle, we are not prepared!

Jesus' ministry was to establish the kingdom of God on earth, liberating creation from the destructive grasp of the adversary. As John says, Jesus came to destroy the works of Satan, the former ruler of this world (1 Jn 3:18). The adversary is the ultimate author of all that disrupts the harmony of God's creation.

Though Satan is defeated through Christ, he is not fully destroyed. He still roams the earth seeking to disrupt the purposes of God. In fact, Scripture tells us that his activities are all the more intense, for he knows that his time is short and his authority is diminished.

QUESTIONS FOR REFLECTION AND DISCUSSION

What is your reaction to this notion that life includes spiritual battles—including confrontations with the adversary?

List some of the primary ways you think the adversary seeks to thwart Christians.

From your memory of the book of Acts, how did the early church confront opposition?

Is there a danger in becoming preoccupied with the adversary?

What would you characterize as a balanced perspective?

SECTION TWO:
THE RESOURCES FOR THE BATTLE

We serve a victorious Savior, and we face a defeated foe. We must never allow our perception of the adversary's power to overshadow our confidence in the sovereign Lord.

God will not send us into the battle without giving us the resources necessary to prevail. The one who is in us is greater than the one who is in the world (1 Jn 4:4). God's strength is made perfect in our weakness (2 Cor 12:9).

The name of Jesus. The first resource God gives us is the liberating awareness that Jesus has been given all authority in heaven and earth. We do not live in a world that is madly out of control. Evil is not without restraint. All things are under Jesus' ultimate authority.

QUESTIONS FOR REFLECTION AND DISCUSSION

Read Matthew 28:18-20 and Luke 9:1-6 or 10:1-20.
How do these verses portray the relationship between Christ's authority, the adversary's opposition and the church's engagement in mission?

God will not send us into the battle without giving us the resources necessary to prevail.

What practical assistance is derived from knowing that we serve through Christ's authority?

How might understanding this truth help you deal with a specific area of opposition you are currently experiencing?

How might it help you deal with an area of opposition you anticipate encountering in your place of service?

The armor of God. We often enter the world wearing only the helmet of salvation, knowing that we are forgiven and saved through Jesus Christ. A helmet is great, but without other armor we are thoroughly unprotected.

God has provided us with all the resources we need to manifest his authority over areas that the adversary seeks to dominate. Knowing how to use these resources is a vital dimension of maturing in Christ and engaging in ministry.

QUESTIONS FOR REFLECTION AND DISCUSSION

Read Ephesians 6:10-20.

How do you feel about the idea that we do not labor against flesh and blood but against principalities and powers?

List the various items of armor, and describe the significance of each for our protection and our penetration of the adversary's dominion.

The power of the Holy Spirit in prayer. We cannot minimize the significance of prayer. Note what Paul says we are to do once we are fully clothed with the armor of God: stand, pray and proclaim Christ.

Prayer is not only our essential communication with the Lord. Prayer is not only our key to receiving resources for engagement in ministry. Prayer is also our most effective form of rebellion against the status quo.

Through prayer we utter God's *no* to the forces of darkness and God's *yes* to the forces of the kingdom of light. Through prayer we agree with God's will that God's kingdom will come and God's will be done on earth with the same fullness as in heaven. Through prayer the power of God is further released for the transformation of the world.

If we are to participate in God's mission in the world, we need to be equipped as intercessors.

One of the most significant ministries we gain from our short-term service is the ability to pray more intelligently and passionately for the region of the world we visited. In prayer we participate in the work of the Holy Spirit. This is one of the highest and holiest dimensions of our calling and vocation as the people of God.

QUESTIONS FOR REFLECTION AND DISCUSSION

Read Matthew 18:18-20.
What do you think Jesus means by "binding and loosing"?

What are we to bind and loose? How?

What experience have you had with this form of prayer?

Consider this quote from *Beyond Duty:* "Perhaps one of the most valuable things I do as a missionary is serve as a conduit of people's prayer for a particular part of the world—drawing other Christians' attention to the conflict between the kingdoms of light and darkness in that region" (p. 81). How can you encourage others' intercession for the region where you will be serving?

In regard to preparation for spiritual battle, how would you like others to pray for you?

SECTION THREE:
BEING NOURISHED BY OUR LIFE IN CHRIST

The gospel weans us of our addictions to circumstances as our source of security and accomplishments as our definition of worth.

When we enter a new culture, the normal props that upheld our sense of security and worth are knocked out from beneath us. Suddenly, the old sources of identity are gone: the acquisitions and accomplishments, the titles and roles, the ability to meet others' expectations, the capacity to have our own expectations fulfilled. No one knows who we are. We're not even sure we know who we are!

This crisis can leave us floundering and grasping for new props to hold up our sagging egos, or it can drive us into deeper intimacy with Christ.

The true adventure of crosscultural ministry is finding Christ in the new situation and participating with him in his ministry there.

Our fruitfulness in ministry and the fruit of the experience in our own lives partially depends on how we answer the question: Do we live in our circumstances, or do we live in Christ?

QUESTIONS FOR REFLECTION AND DISCUSSION

Read Philippians 3:4-15.
What sources of security and worth did Paul have before coming to Christ?

Why was being "found in Christ" of such supreme value to Paul that he was willing to consider everything else rubbish?

Are there things you have difficulty regarding as rubbish, thus placing them above or alongside your relationship with Christ? What are they?

Journaling is a helpful tool for deepening our focus on Christ. Review the following list of guidelines for journaling.

- Don't journal as a duty. Rather, approach it as writing a letter to a beloved friend.

- Begin with "Dear Lord," and then write a letter to God sharing your thoughts, fears, joys and concerns.

- Don't worry about being profound. Journal entries are not your memoirs but a private dialogue with God.

- Incorporate reflections on the Bible. This makes it a true dialogue. Choose one section of Scripture to study throughout your short-term service.

- Conclude by listening to God and expressing your thankfulness. Ask yourself what God may be seeking to say to you.

What has been your experience with journaling?

How might journaling be helpful while on your trip?

There is one more resource that is foundational to growth and fruitfulness in the midst of adversity. It is found in remembering this simple truth: Ultimately, we do not serve people, programs, projects, our own ambitions or others' expectations. It is the Lord Christ whom we serve.

"Whatever you do, do your work heartily, as for the Lord rather than for men, knowing that from the Lord you will receive the reward of the inheritance. It is the Lord Christ whom you serve" (Col 3:23-24 NASB).

We not only serve *in* Christ—in his name, life and power—but we also direct our service *to* Christ. Thus, we return again to the daily prayer of the Missionaries of Charity: "Lord Jesus, when I encounter you today in the unattractive disguise of the irritating, the exacting and the unreasonable, may I still recognize you and say, 'Sweet Jesus, what a privilege to serve you today!'"

QUESTIONS FOR REFLECTION AND DISCUSSION

Read Matthew 25:31-46.
What are some of the "disguises" in which Jesus appears to us?

In your opinion, why does Christ say that service to these people is really service to him?

How does this affect your attitude toward serving people you might normally choose to avoid?

With whom (or in what situation) do you anticipate most needing to see Christ as the object of your service?

SUGGESTED READING AND LEARNING EXERCISES

Language acquisition phrases 14-16, appendix three

eight

PREPARING TO RETURN HOME

Returning home can be harder than going to a new place. When we leave, it is with a great sense of adventure. We anticipate newness, change and challenges. We often go with a team that we've come to appreciate and on which we'll rely. While we're serving, we experience a sense of community and closeness that is hard to find back home. Plus, we feel a special purposefulness, like our lives are really counting for something. Our lives at home, on the other hand, often feel consumed by busyness and activities that lack deep significance. Through our short-term service, our horizons have expanded, our confidence has deepened and our faith in God has grown.

In this chapter we will prepare ourselves for what to expect when returning home so that this experience can be as fruitful as possible.

SUGGESTED GROUP ACTIVITY

As people enter the room, have them write several questions that they would like to be asked by a debriefing partner. Discuss these questions together as a group, then discuss the qualities of a good debriefing partner.

SECTION ONE:
FROM CULTURE FATIGUE TO CULTURE GRIEF

We're excited about returning home, looking forward to lattes and water straight from the faucet. We're glad to sleep in our own bed and to enjoy a private bathroom. Life in our own country certainly seems safer, more certain and more stable than what we experienced. But that also makes returning home harder than we thought.

People forgot we were gone. Life here has gone on just as usual. In fact, many people hardly seem to have noticed that we were gone. "I haven't seen you for a while," they may say. "Have you been on a trip or something?" When we tell them where we've been, all they say is, "Oh, that must have been great. Did you have a good time?" The conversation is quickly redirected to the status of the local sports team or the latest movie. You've just had one of the most life-changing experiences of your life, and all people seem to ask is, "How was it?" What are you supposed to say? "Fine"?

Added to people's seeming disinterest in your trip is the frustration that you will inevitably feel over certain aspects of life in the West. Everything seems so fast, so busy, so glitzy, so expensive, so lonely, so extravagant.

We don't have time to reflect. Often we have to return immediately to school or work without much opportunity to reflect on what we saw, experienced, felt and learned. Amidst the press of responsibilities, our short-term service soon becomes precisely what we vowed it wouldn't—a distant memory.

We're gripped by culture grief. Culture shock is a normal part of entering into a new culture. The dislocation of entering into an unfamiliar world can produce a shock that even has physical manifestations. We lose our bearings, become disoriented and are unsure how to move forward. With time, we adjust and learn how to live effectively in the new context, becoming personally enriched through the process.

Many people experience a similar shock when they return home, usually called "reverse culture shock." What we thought would be familiar now seems strange. We've changed, and our perspectives have changed. It's like entering a new world again. If we've been gone long enough, what once was home may have changed too. We're not sure how we fit in. The same shock of adjustment takes over.

However, culture shock doesn't adequately describe the challenges of reentry. It's more a form of culture grief. We feel saddened and dismayed by what we encounter at home. Our lives seemed more meaningful when we were on our short-term mission trip. We seemed more in touch with the important issues of life, more surrounded by a caring community. Now we enter into Western culture's loneliness, busyness and materialism. Not only are we unsure how to navigate this, we're not even sure we want to.

QUESTIONS FOR REFLECTION AND DISCUSSION

What is your reaction to this portrayal of challenges you may face, when returning home?

If you have been on a short-term mission trip before, how does this portrayal compare to your previous experience?

What do you think will help you to adjust?

Discuss with someone who has already been on a crosscultural trip what helped them to reenter.

Prepare now to communicate then. As mentioned in chapter three, before leaving it is valuable to pray about our trip and how we will relay the experience when we return. Be praying now that God will help you to recognize

- one or two people with whom he would have you maintain a relationship after you return home
- one situation you encounter that encapsulates your experience

Describing these people or this situation to others on your return (usually in three or four minutes) is an excellent way to help others enter into your experience. This might stimulate their curiosity about your trip and help them to know what other questions they could ask.

SECTION TWO:
THE COMMON PROCESS OF READJUSTMENT AND REENTRY

The first thing to remember as you reenter life at home is that what you will experience is common to most people who've had meaningful crosscultural encounters. It is as valuable a part of your experience as the trip itself.

Figure 8.1 illustrates the cycle you may go through emotionally and the stages of adjustment to reentry.

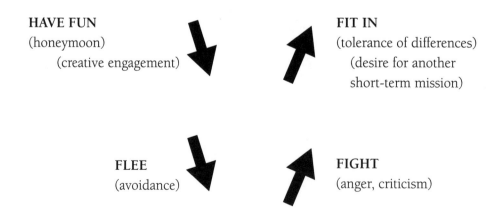

HAVE FUN
(honeymoon)
   (creative engagement)

FIT IN
(tolerance of differences)
   (desire for another
   short-term mission)

FLEE
(avoidance)

FIGHT
(anger, criticism)

Figure 8.1. Adapted from Lisa Espineli Chinn, *Reentry Guide for Short-Term Mission Leaders* (Orlando: DeeperRoots, 1998), p. 14. Used by permission.

Fun.

- "I can't wait for a hot shower."
- "Oh, the delight of sleeping in my own bed."
- "I really missed you."
- "I never thought a hamburger would taste so good."

You're glad to be home. It's great looking at pictures of your trip. You feel changed in your life, in your relationship with God and in your vision of the world. You're ready to do things differently.

Flee.

- "No one seems to be interested in my experience. They only ask me 'How was your trip?'"
- "Everyone here is so busy. Life seems so fast."
- "I hate the freeways."
- "I really miss my team."

You're discouraged by how materialistic, impersonal and busy life here seems to be. You feel alone and miss the community you experienced with your team. People here seem to be preoccupied with petty concerns and easily depressed by silly issues—especially when compared to the faith, joy and community you witnessed on your trip. You wish you could return. Somehow life felt more real, more solid, more significant there than it does here. Because you can't return, you find yourself spending lots of time reliving memories, looking at pictures and trying to make contact with your team members. Even that is difficult because both you and they are being swept up in the pressure and busyness of life here.

Fight.

- "People seem to take their faith so much more seriously over there. . ."
- "My church service seems so passionless."
- "People are more interested in expanding their savings account than in saving the lost."
- "We live as such isolated individuals. God calls us to intimate community."

You find yourself actually feeling depressed. People here seem

indifferent to the real issues in life. Even the church fosters a self-indulgent, self-preoccupied spirituality. Money dominates everything. You're becoming highly critical of life at home, and you speak out against what you see. When you're silent you find yourself feeling spiritually superior, as if your understanding is better than others'.

Fit.

- "I can't live here like people do there. I tried to live differently, but it's impossible."

- "The cost of living is so much higher here. I have to accept it."

- "I have to return to my normal responsibilities. I can't just drop everything. I've got so much that I have to do."

- "I'm losing my friends because they see me as a 'mission fanatic.'"

The pressure to fit in. Now you find yourself simply seeking to fit in. The press of responsibilities has taken hold, and it's simply too hard to keep focused on your experience over there. The memories are beginning to fade, and you haven't been able to find ways to live differently in light of what you've experienced. You promised you'd write the people you visited, but you've barely had time to send a postcard.

The longing for another short-term mission trip. You find yourself longing for another short-term mission trip. Maybe that will help you recapture the feeling of significance that you experienced before. Maybe that will stimulate your spiritual growth and draw you back into a sense of community.

An aborted process. Unfortunately, many people end the reentry process here. Their trip becomes a distant memory. They feel a nagging guilt over not being able to live differently in light of what they learned. But other than giving money to mission projects, praying occasionally for the people they met and looking forward to another short-term trip, they don't know what else they can do.

SECTION THREE:
MOVING INTO FRUITFULNESS AND JOURNEY-ING THROUGH LIFE'S GREAT QUESTIONS

God wants to lead you into life-transforming, creative fruitfulness through what you experienced and learned. In your spiritual life, your lifestyle, your relationships, your vocation and the expression of your global citizenship, God has rich and wonderful fruit to express through you.

Your trip may be over, but a new journey has begun. In fact, the second journey may be one of the primary reasons why God called you to go on the first one. As was mentioned in the first chapter, a good short-term, crosscultural mission experience opens our lives up to the "Eight Great Questions." The quality, extent and durability of the fruit in your life will partially depend on your engagement with these questions. Being led by the Spirit of God down the path of fruitfulness will take effort and time. Thus, your journey from mission tourism to global citizenship continues long after you return home.

Remember, you are building a life for the rest of your life. Therefore, it's essential to be patient and persistent. You may spend several months walking through these questions. Personally, these are questions I face daily, and even twenty years later I am still reflecting on my short-term mission experiences. The following tips will help you in this process.

Continue to keep a journal. Write in the form of letters to God, talking with God about what you are feeling, experiencing and thinking as you reenter.

Write reflections on the "Eight Great Questions." Objectify your thoughts by writing them down. The remainder of this chapter will be a set of reflection questions.

Discuss your reflections with others. Optimally, you might talk with your team members, another group of people reentering their home country from a short-term mission experience, a prayer partner or your spouse. You may want to make a commitment to meet monthly for several months after you return. Merely gathering to share photos and swap stories won't be sufficient. Enjoy abundant time with your debriefing partner. Encourage this person to listen to your reflections on these eight questions, as well as any others that seem pertinent.

Be patient. You are in this for the long-term process—actually, for eternity. Therefore, allow yourself time as you work through this. Be patient not only with yourself but with others, who don't always understand you like you would want.

Your trip may be over, but a new journey has begun. In fact, the second journey may be one of the primary reasons why God called you to go on the first one.

One more time—keep a journal. Sound repetitive? Chronicle your pilgrimage. Give yourself time to enjoy long dialogues with God. God is the author of this quest, and the author and perfecter of your faith. Keep God as a participant in the process.

THE EIGHT GREAT QUESTIONS

Who am I? What have I learned about myself?

I have changed. Some of these changes are temporary, necessary adjustments to my short-term mission experience. Others are permanent changes that God wants to weave into the fabric of my life. While on my trip, I faced the issue of my own identity. What gives me a sense of worth and significance?

I have experienced new forms of conflict. Often the stress of a trip leads to significant conflict both with teammates and people in the community. What have I learned about forgiveness and conflict resolution?

I have experienced myself in new ways. What surprised me about myself while on the trip? What strengths and gifts do I see God developing in me?

Who is God? How has my understanding of God changed?

I may have encountered some of the other major world religions in new ways. How does the Christian faith relate to other faiths? What did I encounter in people of other faiths that surprised me? What did I see that I valued? How would I answer the question of whether devout people in other faiths need to believe in Christ?

I may have seen forms of worship that are new to me. What is my understanding of spiritual gifts, especially speaking in tongues and the pursuit of miraculous signs and wonders? What is the place of diverse forms of worship in the church?

My encounter with poverty, injustice and suffering may have raised some questions in my life. How do I reconcile the sovereign goodness of God with the suffering in the world?

Who are we? What have I learned about community?

I have experienced new forms of dependency as well as hospitality. What have I learned about how to be a part of a welcoming community? How do I want to treat strangers in light of how I was treated?

I may have experienced tension in interpersonal relationships. What have I learned about teamwork, confrontation, forgiveness and reconciliation?

I long for the same sense of community I experienced on the trip. How should I alter my lifestyle in order to make more room for people? What commitment do I want to make to maintain some of the relationships I built on this trip—through prayer, correspondence and interaction with teammates and crosscultural friends?

I find myself critical of life here. How can I use the changes in me to build bridges that will draw others into a deeper encounter with Christ and a deeper engagement with God's work in the world? How can I avoid simply being an irritant in people's lives, alienating them from me, from God and from mission?

What is the impact of culture on faith? How do I see life and the gospel differently because of what I've experienced?

I have seen radically different ways of life. What have I learned about the impact of culture on faith? What do I see in my understanding of the Christian life that has been formed more by living in America than by the gospel?

I have encountered different ways of dealing with the Bible. How do I read Scripture differently after my short-term experience? How do I discern between what is biblical and what is merely cultural in our Christian practices and understanding? How do I decide what in a culture is neutral in relation to the gospel and what needs to be changed?

I have seen many ways in which cultures are changing. How can a culture be encouraged to change in ways that are life-giving and consistent with the gospel, rather than in ways that are destructive?

What's wrong with the world? Why is there such suffering and injustice in it?

I have encountered new forms of suffering. What have I learned about the causes of suffering? What is the role of society, the environment, the Adversary and individuals themselves? What are helpful and immediate ways to respond to people in distress? What are ways to address the structural causes of suffering?

I have seen new forms of corruption and injustice. What are effective ways to address injustice in the world? What would God seek

to do through the church? To what extent are international entities (governments, corporations, etc.) responsible for injustice? What is the role of my own country?

What does it mean to be a follower of Christ? What have I learned about discipleship?

I felt closer to God there than I do here. Why? Why was it so much easier to spend time in prayer and Bible study there than it is now? Why am I so undisciplined here?

I encountered people with great joy in circumstances that would utterly depress me. Why can people in contexts of poverty seem to live with such vibrant joy?

I encountered people with a wholehearted commitment to Christ. Why were people there willing to pay a high price for their faith, while in my own country we tend to expect a high benefit from ours? What have I learned that I want to incorporate into my own life as a disciple of Christ?

What's of value? How do I live here in light of what I've seen there?

I encountered people whose way of life was radically different from mine. What questions have been raised for me regarding our lifestyle as Westerners? What really is necessary for happiness? Why does everyone else in the world seem to want to live like we do, yet we often seem so unhappy? What are five or six central values that I would like God to enable me to live out in my lifestyle? What would I want others to say is characteristic of my lifestyle?

I want to live appropriately here in light of what I've seen there. How would I feel if someone from there came to spend a week with me here as my guest? How would they feel? What are several simple, realistic, doable changes I want to make in my lifestyle?

Where am I going? What is God calling me to be and to do as a result of this experience?

I felt a deep sense of significance while on this trip. How can my life count for the kingdom of God? I want to make a difference in the world and not just wait for my next short-term mission trip to feel a sense of adventure and significance. If I could dream big for how God might want to work through me, what would I dream?

I encountered my gifts (and limitations) in new ways. What has God entrusted me with that I could use in God's service? How do I want to develop and enhance these gifts? Are they currently fully employed for God? Why or why not? What might God be calling me to do differently?

I feel a deep desire and sense of responsibility to help others learn from what I've experienced. If I could summarize the impact of this trip on my life and what I think God would have people in my own country do in response to the needs of the people I met, what would I say? How can I communicate this message to others? How can I encourage others to join me in regular, crosscultural prayer?

What steps do I want to take to explore more fully what God might want to do through me? Do I need further training? Do I need to discover what opportunities might be available? With whom do I need to discuss this?

What barriers keep me from refocusing my sense of vocation? Why is this difficult for me? How can these difficulties be surmounted?

Based on your interaction with these questions, what would you want to include in a mission statement for your life here? You wrote a mission statement for your short-term service. Now you have the opportunity to write one for your long-term service.

May God bless and encourage you in the delightful adventure of living through God's grace and Spirit as a global citizen.

SUGGESTED READING AND LEARNING EXERCISES

Mack and Leeann's Guide to Short-Term Missions, chapter 18

LEADER'S GUIDE
FOR EACH CHAPTER

The following information is intended for team leaders or trainers preparing groups for crosscultural experiences.

Before your first training meeting, we suggest you have a time for team members to learn about the trip, ask questions, go over a to-do list (including getting a passport, immunizations and strategies for raising financial support), be introduced to their team and learn about the orientation process. Some team members may question the value of investing so much time in orientation, especially those who have been on other short-term mission trips without this kind of preparation. Encourage them to approach this time of preparation as an opportunity to deepen their understanding of the gospel, of God's mission in the world and of crosscultural ministry.

Invite them to go on a pilgrimage. This pilgrimage in short-term mission has four phases: preparation, the time of service, integration and debriefing after returning, and the ongoing impact on the coming years of their lives.

Stress with your group the conviction that underlies this workbook: the quality of the impact of their short-term service on the people they are serving and on their own lives will be a direct function of the quality of their preparation and debriefing. Make sure everyone

- has a copy of the workbook as well as any other books you are using (*Beyond Duty, Mack and Leeann's Guide to Short-Term Missions*)

- understands that most chapters are divided into three sections, each involving about an hour of work (so they should plan on three to four hours of preparation per week)

- is aware of the supplemental activities that you are incorporating—language acquisition phrases, church visits, context/country research, etc.

Group activities and discussion and reflection suggestions are provided for each chapter of the workbook. They are designed for a 90-minute weekly session.

- 10 to 40 minutes: group activity
- 20 to 30 minutes: lecture or overview of the chapter (a CD containing PowerPoint presentations is available from the author; e-mail him at tdearborn@ivpress.com.)
- 30 minutes: discussion and prayer

At the conclusion of each week's discussion it may be helpful to devote some time to logistical details: travel, finances, health and specific training for the service you'll be providing.

o n e
THE GOD OF MISSION

This first session will set a tone for your entire time of preparation. You want to build an atmosphere of confidence in God and of the freedom to be honest with one another; you also want to lay the foundations for your group to become a supportive community.

1. If your group doesn't know one another, begin with the simple getting acquainted exercise outlined in the workbook (10 min.).

2. Follow this up with the "Insiders-Outsiders" simulation game (30 min., see instructions below).

3. Following the game, offer your summary of the kingdom of God as the integrating theme for engagement in mission (see author's PowerPoint CD). Then ask the group for their reflections on the statement, "The church of God does not have a mission in the world. The God of mission has a church in the world!" (15 min.).

4. In the context of studying Acts 1, ask your group what it means for them to be engaged in full-time Christian service. How does this impact the common notion that when we go on a short-term mission trip, we're giving two weeks (or two months) to serve the Lord (5 min.)?

5. Discuss as a group the "Eight Great Questions." These form the foundation of this preparation workbook and are the guide for participants' journaling while on the trip and debriefing when they return. Ask people to discuss in small groups how they feel about the idea that their own learning is an important aspect of the trip. Ask them to discuss which question most intrigues them (15 min.).

6. As you draw to a conclusion, encourage people to begin praying about who would be a good debriefing partner. Also have team members divide up aspects of the culture/country research questions listed in appendix three. Each person should prepare a brief presentation for the whole team. The other long-term preparation project pertains to language acquisition. Talk with your team about the language acquisition phrases, and decide if and how you will learn them. Finally, discuss what you would like to do to meet people who are, or attend a church in your area that is, representative of the people or language group where you will be going (10 min.).

7. End by having people describe how the final quotation in this chapter from P. T. Forsyth affects their attitude as they approach this short-term mission trip. Then pray together based on Paul's statement in 1 Corinthians 2—that we might see Christ crucified among the people we are going to serve (5 min.).

Instructions for the "Insiders-Outsiders" simulation game. Allow thirty minutes for the entire activity depending on the size of your group (larger groups will take longer). The purpose of the game is to offer insight into how we may be perceived or how we may feel as visitors in another culture (but don't tell your team this at the beginning).

How to play the game. Split the team evenly into two groups. Take the outsiders to another location nearby but out of sight and earshot from the insiders. Give each group cultural "rules" to follow.

Rules for the insiders. You are a group of friendly, touchy, laid back and generally gregarious people. You have a group of visitors coming, and you are to make them feel welcome and show them a nice time. You want them to feel comfortable and to have a good impression of your culture. In your culture, it is very rude for a man to approach a woman, and the men are protectors of the women. You do not speak English (make up gibberish to talk to one another). However, you answer every question asked by your visitors with the words "Yes," "Sure" and a smile.

Rules for the outsiders. You are a group of purpose-driven and highly effective people. You pride yourselves on the fact that you can move into a situation, assess it and make positive changes. You have been given a mission: Go into this strange group of people and find out why they are not productive, offering suggestions and solutions for problems in their community. You know there are at least two big problems, but part of your mission is to first identify these problems.

Game time. Give each group their rules, and allow them to practice with each other for a minute before sending the outsiders in to meet the insiders. Allow enough game time for people to interact with several people from the other group (about 5 min.).

When you see that the game is breaking down, have everyone sit in a circle for a discussion time. The purpose of the debriefing is to find similarities between the game experience and what can happen in short-term missions when Westerners move into a situation, assume there are problems and attempt to fix things in their own manner. Begin by exploring what this experience felt like to both the insiders and the outsiders.

Debriefing questions.

- Insiders, what did this experience feel like for you?
- Outsiders, what was your experience like?
- You were each given rules for your group—can anyone guess the other group's rules? (Allow several guesses before allowing each group to disclose their rules.)
- Insiders, what were your reactions to the outsiders? How might this apply to the culture we are going to?
- Outsiders, how did you react to the insiders? How might your experience apply to the trip we are planning to take?
- What are some other experiences or feelings you had? How might these apply to our upcoming experience on this mission trip?

t w o
LEARNING TO DELIGHT IN DIFFERENCES

Have fun with this chapter. It's a great opportunity to have people tell stories of embarrassing crosscultural incidents they've been in or read about. One of the keys to enjoying life in a new culture is to be able to laugh at ourselves and overcome our fear of looking foolish.

1. The "Church Game" provides an opportunity to discuss ways our cultural experience affects our view of church. Discuss ways in which church life may be different in the community where you are going (10 min.).

2. In response to the section on stereotypes, it might be fun to organize in advance a skit portraying "the ugly American tourist." Encourage several people to let their creative imaginations run wild with this. Then discuss stereotypes that people in your group may have of those in the community where they will serve, as well as stereotypes they may have of Westerners (10 min.).

   Another way to address this same theme is to distribute large pieces of paper and colored pens, asking people to either draw a picture of how they envision life to be like where they're going or to list words describing their preconceptions of the people and their lifestyle. Discuss the implications of Goldschmidt's idea that people are more alike than their cultures and the assertion that we're actually encountering long-lost distant relatives (15 min.).

3. Present a definition of culture and a summary of the role culture plays in our lives (15 min., see author's PowerPoint CD).

4. In small groups, invite people to describe common sayings or adages on which they were raised and to describe how these contributed to their sense of right and wrong. Then discuss this as a group (10 min.).

5. Since it's natural to judge other cultures according to the values of our own culture, and since we tend to regard our own values as biblical, it's important to linger over the exercises in section two. Discuss the criteria people used to determine if certain behaviors were biblical, contextual or universal (15 min.).

6. Equally important as our criteria is our attitude. Have people describe their reflections on Philippians 2, and discuss how we can have the mind or attitude of Christ (10 min.).

7. Discuss people's evaluations of the cultural worldview grid. Are there differing viewpoints within your group? Discuss again the criteria people used in making their evaluations (10 min.).

8. Conclude by asking people to summarize what they think are the keys to effectively entering into a new culture. Encourage people to suggest prayer requests regarding this, and pray for the people whom you will be serving (10 min.).

three
EMBRACING CHANGE

This chapter provides an opportunity to personalize some of the challenges of entering into a new culture. Crosscultural living and communication is a learned skill. Some learn it more easily than others. Encourage people to identify their strengths and their challenges when it comes to adjusting to a context where things are different and unfamiliar.

1. If you have time, begin by playing the "Castaways on a Desert Island" simulation game (30 min., see instructions below).

2. In small groups, have people share their personal trauma score as well as the picture they drew portraying their feelings about cultural fatigue and stressful situations. Discuss other situations you will encounter that might be difficult (15 min.).

3. Discuss the five dimensions of G.R.A.C.E.: Gratitude, Refreshment, Acceptance, Compassion and Expectancy (30 min., see author's PowerPoint CD).

   • What are people's reactions to the notion that complaint and criticism create a bottomless pit?

   • Is it unrealistic to be thankful for all things?

   • In small groups, have people describe

      situations in which thankfulness has transformed their response to hardship

      patterns they would like to commit themselves to in order to maintain rhythm and refreshment

      their ideas of what God might want to accomplish in and through them

4. Give people time by themselves to write down ideas they would like to include in their personal mission statement for the trip (10 min.).

5. Conclude by praying together that God would indeed give you G.R.A.C.E. as you encounter new and challenging situations (5 min.).

Instructions for "Castaways on a Desert Island" simulation game. Divide people into groups of five or six, and give them a section of the room as their island. Give each group a pen and paper, and tell them they have ten minutes to write the constitution for their island. This should include a name for the island, someone selected to be its ruler, three rules and a penalty for disobeying the rules. Suggest that rules could pertain to things like who can initiate conversation (men or women), the distance that must be maintained between people during a conversation, gestures used in greeting, the position people must be in when spoken to by the ruler or other aspects of social interaction. Examples of penalties include ignoring someone, speaking to them constantly, making them wear a sign, and assigning someone to hold their hand.

Give each island three minutes to practice their new culture. Now select one person from each group, and send them to a foreign island as a shipwreck castaway. Tell each castaway privately (without the islanders knowing) that they are to discern the rules of the new island (without simply asking people what they are) and then intentionally ignore or seek to change a rule. Allow each island to play for ten minutes.

Gather as a whole to debrief for seven minutes. How hard was it for the castaways to learn the rules? What did it feel like both to be a newcomer and to receive a newcomer who didn't act properly? What happened when they tried to change a rule? Any observations about how you adjust to an unfamiliar context when you don't know the rules?

four
MAXIMIZING PERSONAL GROWTH

This chapter provides opportunities to carry personal assessment to an even deeper level. Hopefully by now your group has developed a safe atmosphere of mutual trust and respect.

1. As people enter have them add their thoughts to two lists on the board: one of common fears about crosscultural ministry and one of the qualities of a good missionary.

2. In small groups, have people describe what they checked on their lists of expectations and fears. What did people write regarding how their teammates can best assist them when they are feeling anxious? Invite people to share which of the "Eight Great Questions" seems most pressing in their life as they anticipate the trip. Also have everyone share their answers to the personal mission statement questions (20 min.).

3. In the same small group discuss the qualities of a good missionary. How did people rate themselves? What do people perceive to be the strengths they bring to a crosscultural situation? Pray together in small groups (15 min.).

4. Divide people into eight new groups, and have each group examine one of the common Western values and its biblical response. Have each group read the biblical passages for their section. They should discuss their personal experiences with this particular value and the gospel alternative. What has helped the biblical value penetrate more fully into their lives? In what ways do they still feel the need to grow in this area?

   Gather as a whole, and discuss people's observations from this discussion (25 min., see author's PowerPoint CD).

5. Conclude your time by having people share what they've learned through the culture/country research project. Then discuss how this has enhanced their expectations for the trip. End by praying for the context where you will be serving (30 min.).

five
WORKING TOGETHER AS A TEAM

The goal of this session is for people to discern the dynamics they each bring to the team and to discuss how their team can best work together.

1. Play the two team exercises, and enjoy the debriefing process as an entire group (25 min.).

2. As teams, have people discuss the positive and negative team experiences they have had, the helpful qualities they bring to their

team and something their team should know about them to en-hance their life together (20 min.).

3. "Section Two: Expanding Your Team" is especially important to discuss, since the very reason for going on this trip involves in-corporating people in your new context into your life (see au-thor's PowerPoint CD).

- Read John 17 aloud as a group, and discuss the implications of the kind of oneness for which Jesus prays.

- Invite people to describe their own experience with journal-ing and what it would mean to use their journal as a "gar-bage dump" for frustrations and criticisms.

- Discuss what it would mean to view people in your new context as co-heirs with you (20 min.).

4. Conclude by having each team draft the components of their team covenant. Each team should select two people to meet dur-ing the week and refine it (20 min.).

5. End by praying for each team.

six
COMMUNICATING CLEARLY

God is the master communicator, capable of speaking to every hu-man heart in its own context, culture and language.

1. The "Bridges and Bombs" exercise is a great way to introduce the challenges of communication. Few people are good listeners, and this is especially true in short-term mission as we feel pressured to get the Word out as fast as possible (20 min.).

2. In small groups, have people discuss situations in which they or others arrived late to a meeting or activity. What was helpful in that situation? What was unhelpful? Discuss the concept that in short-term mission we are arriving late to an ongoing conversa-tion between people and God (15 min.).

3. Have fun with the section of Christian clichés. Invite people to list words or phrases in addition to the ones mentioned in the workbook. Discuss ways that these clichés could be rephrased so as not to be misunderstood (15 min.).

4. In pairs, ask people to talk about what they learned as they wrote

and rewrote their testimonies. Encourage them to read their testimonies to each other and discuss how each one could be made more clear (15 min.).

5. Summarize for the group some of the keys for effective communication listed in the workbook (15 min., see author's PowerPoint CD).

6. Conclude by having people discuss in small groups what they learned from their study of Paul's sermons and what they think God needs to overcome in them to enhance their effectiveness as a communicator of the gospel. Have them pray for one another (10 min.).

seven
STAYING SPIRITUALLY FRESH

Reproduce the bookmark in appendix four. Print the prayer of the Missionaries of Charity on one side of the bookmark and Galatians 2:19-20 on the other. You might want to print it on bright paper and have it laminated for durability. You'll use the other material in the appendix, "Eight Great Questions" and "Twelve Insights," in the next session.

1. As people enter, give them the bookmark. Encourage everyone to pray and meditate on the prayer of the Missionaries of Charity and on Galatians 2:20. Suggest that people use the bookmark in their Bibles during the trip (10 min.).

2. Some people in your group may be surprised by this chapter's discussion of spiritual battle and the adversary. Discuss people's reactions to this topic and what they learned from the Bible about Christ's authority, the adversary's authority, and what it means for us to live in Christ (30 min., see author's PowerPoint CD).

3. In Paul's discussion of the armor of God he says we are to do three things—stand in the face of opposition, pray and proclaim Christ. Central to life and mission is intercessory prayer. In small groups, invite people to discuss their experience with intercessory prayer. Has it been easy or difficult? Why? What have they found to be helpful (10 min.)?

4. One of the gifts we give people on short-term mission trips is the ability to pray for them more intelligently and intentionally than

we could have before. Those who support us also pray with an earnestness and specificity they might not have had before.

- Discuss what commitment you want to make as a team to encourage one another in personal and corporate times of prayer and Bible study while on the trip.

- Have people list on the board the names of their prayer/debriefing partners. Invest a few minutes in prayer for these people.

- Discuss how you can keep these partners informed of prayer needs while you are gone without being disrespectful toward the people whom you will be serving (20 min.).

5. Discuss again what commitment you would like to make as a team to encourage one another to remain spiritually fresh. How can you pray, study the Bible, worship and journal in a way that is not exclusionary of your hosts or rude (10 min.)?

6. Conclude by discussing what it means to see Christ in disguise. How can this impact how we relate to people, even unpleasant people? Pray the Missionaries of Charity's daily prayer aloud together (10 min.).

eight
PREPARING TO RETURN HOME

For many people, the hardest part of a short-term mission trip begins when they arrive back home. Preparing for return is as important as preparing for departure.

1. Begin by discussing good debriefing questions and the qualities of a good debriefing partner. Invite several people to role play re-entry, with you acting out the person who gives uninterested responses or asks unhelpful questions (15 min.).

2. Ask those who've gone on short-term mission trips before what their experiences were with culture grief and what helped them to readjust. Discuss the chart detailing the common readjustment and reentry process. Ask people what will help them to creatively engage with life back home in light of what they experienced (10 min., see author's PowerPoint CD).

3. Distribute the laminated reproductions of the "Eight Great Questions" and "Twelve Insights" from appendix four. In small groups, invite people to discuss the following:

- Which question most intrigues them?

- Do any make them apprehensive?

- How do they feel about the idea that their attitudes, beliefs and desired behaviors may change as a result of this trip?

- How might others who are important in their life respond to the possibility that they may change?

(It is important to note that not all short-term mission experiences are life-transforming. If people don't change at all, that won't make the trip a failure. Rather, it may be God's affirmation of the health of their life as it is.) Encourage people to keep the copy of the "Eight Great Questions" in their journal, along with their personal mission statement and team covenant. They should refer to them frequently throughout the trip (20 min.).

4. Remind people of some of the objectives for short-term trips suggested in chapter three.

- To continue to pray specifically for that context after you've returned

- To develop one or two relationships that you will continue through prayer, correspondence and maybe even e-mail or an occasional phone call

- To leave a legacy of affirmation among people in that context

Conclude with an extensive time of prayer for each person, commissioning them for this team and this trip.

5. Go over any final logistical information that you need to discuss.

RECOMMENDED READING, ADDITIONAL RESOURCES AND WEBSITES

Dearborn, Tim. *Beyond Duty: A Passion for Christ, a Heart for Mission.* Monrovia, Calif.: MARC, 1998.

Stiles, J. Mack, and Leeann Stiles. *Mack and Leeann's Guide to Short-Term Mission.* Downers Grove, Ill.: InterVarsity Press, 2000.

ORGANIZING FOR SHORT-TERM MISSION SERVICE

Forward, David C. *The Essential Guide for the Short Term Mission Trip.* Chicago: Moody Press, 1998.

Gibson, Tim, Steve Hawthorne, Richard Krekel, and Ken Moy, eds. *Stepping Out: The Essential Guide to Short Term Mission.* Seattle: YWAM, 1992.

Judge, Cindy. *Before You Pack Your Bag Prepare Your Heart: 12 Bible Studies for Short-Term Mission Preparation.* Wheaton, Ill.: Campfire Resources, 2000.

Tanin, Vicki, Jim Hill, and Roy Howard. *Sending Out Servants: A Church-Based Short-Term Mission Strategy.* Atlanta: ACMC, 1995.

ADJUSTING TO LIFE IN A NEW CULTURE

Engelsviken, Tormod. *Spiritual Conflict in Today's Mission.* Occasional Paper No. 29. Monrovia, Calif.: Lausanne Committee for World Evangelization, 2001.

Kohls, L. Robert. *Survival Kit for Overseas Living.* Yarmouth, Maine: Intercultural Press, 1996.

Larson, Donald, and William Smalley. *Becoming Bilingual: A Guide to Language Learning.* Pasadena, Calif.: William Carey Library, 1972.

Lingenfelter, Sherwood, and Marvin Mayers. *Ministering Crossculturally*. Grand Rapids, Mich.: Baker, 1986.

Loss, Myron. *Culture Shock*. Winona Lake, Ind.: Light and Life Press, 1983.

Storti, Craig. *The Art of Crossing Cultures*. Yarmouth, Maine: Intercultural Press, 1990.

Ward, Ted. *Living Overseas: A Book of Preparations*. New York: Free Press, 1984.

REENTRY

Chinn, Lisa Espineli. *Reentry Guide for Short-term Mission Leaders*. Orlando: Deeper Roots, 1998.

Jordan, Peter. *Re-Entry: Making the Transition from Missions to Life at Home*. Lynnwood, Wash.: YWAM, 1992.

Lisech, Howard, and Bonnie Lisech. *Fishers of Men Reentry Guide: Bible Studies for Those Returning from Career or Short-Term Overseas Service*. Orlando: Deeper Roots, 1997.

INTRODUCTION TO MISSION AND EVANGELISM

Adeney, Miriam. *God's Foreign Policy*. Grand Rapids, Mich.: Eerdmans, 1984.

Chandler, Paul-Gordon. *God's Global Mosaic: What We Can Learn from Christians Around the World*. Downers Grove, Ill.: InterVarsity Press, 2000.

Pippert, Rebecca Manley. *Out of the Saltshaker and into the World*. Downers Grove, Ill.: InterVarsity Press, 1998.

Stackhouse, Max, Tim Dearborn, and Scott Paeth. *The Local Church in a Global Era*. Grand Rapids, Mich.: Eerdmans, 2000.

RELATION OF GOSPEL AND CULTURE

Bosch, David. *Transforming Mission: Paradigm Shifts in the Theology of Mission*. Maryknoll, N.Y.: Orbis, 1991.

Bradshaw, Bruce. *Change Across Cultures*. Grand Rapids, Mich.: Baker, 2002.

Christian, Jayakumar. *God of the Empty-Handed: Poverty, Power and the Kingdom of God*. Monrovia, Calif.: MARC, 1999.

Hesselgrave, David. *Communicating Christ Crossculturally*. Grand Rapids, Mich.: Zondervan, 1978.

Hesselgrave, David. *Planting Churches Crossculturally.* Grand Rapids, Mich.: Baker, 1980.

Hiebert, Paul. *Anthropological Insights for Missionaries.* Grand Rapids, Mich.: Baker, 1985.

Loewen, Jacob. *Culture and Human Values: Christian Intervention in Anthropological Perspective.* Pasadena, Calif.: William Carey Library, 1975.

Luzbetak, Louis. *The Church and Cultures.* Maryknoll, N.Y.: Orbis, 1988.

Mayers, Marvin. *Christianity Confronts Culture: A Strategy for Crosscultural Evangelism.* Grand Rapids, Mich.: Zondervan, 1974.

Samuel, Vinay, and Chris Sugden. *Sharing Jesus in the Two-Thirds World.* Bangalore, India: Partnership in Mission, 1984.

Spencer, Aida Besancon, and William David Spencer. *The Global God: Multicultural Evangelical Views of God.* Grand Rapids, Mich.: Baker, 1998.

CROSSCULTURAL SIMULATION GAMES

Simulations are highly effective tools in preparing people for short-term mission. In addition to the simulations already described in this workbook, the following are also excellent. Note that each is copyrighted and must be purchased from its distributor.

Aid to Minorians (Intercultural Sourcebook). Participants are divided into two groups: The Minorians are a poor and underdeveloped society; while the Majorians are a wealthy society planning a project to help the Minorians.

Bafa Bafa (Simulation Training Systems). Participants are divided into two cultures and are asked to travel back and forth between them. This simulation shows how easy it is to misinterpret actions and exchanges when the rules are unfamiliar. It also demonstrates the need for thought-out strategies when learning about a new culture. "Bafa Bafa" is an outstanding, complex (and expensive) simulation game.

Barnga (Intercultural Press). A nonverbal exercise in which participants are divided into groups to learn a card game based on a number of simple rules. What the participants do not know is that each group's set of rules is slightly different, so when they begin to play the game, conflict develops. As players are not allowed to talk, they must rely on other means of communication.

Brief Encounters (HRD Press). This game explores how people perceive cultural differences. It develops concepts and skills such as enculturation, ethnocentrism, first impressions and interacting with culturally different groups.

Crisis (Simulation Training Systems). Participants form teams, and each team is instructed to manage the affairs of a fictional nation. The nations vary in their resources, strengths and weaknesses, but all must work together to solve an international conflict.

The East-West Game (Intercultural Sourcebook, Volume 1). This simulation focuses on the different cultural assumptions and values of different groups, as one group tries to obtain a valued object from another.

Heelotia (Simulation Training Systems). This game is similar to "Bafa Bafa" but easier to conduct. The cultural rules are intentionally vague so as to make participants decide cultural rules on their own. It looks at how decisions are made and how people interact with another culture group.

Hostage Crisis (Moorehead Kennedy Institute). Terrorists threaten to harm U.S. hostages unless their demands are met. As the demands are not feasible, negotiations become critical. The main themes in this game are Middle Eastern nationalism, issues of justice and crosscultural understanding.

IDE-GO (Intercultural Sourcebook, Volume 1). One group simulates North American culture while another simulates South American culture. This game is designed to provide insight into the interaction processes and behaviors of these two groups.

The Malonarian Cultural Expedition Team (Meridian House International). Participants form a team of cultural anthropologists from the Republic of Malonaria. The team's assignment is to study the United States in order to prepare for educational and diplomatic exchanges between the two cultures. Members of the team are asked to compare American and Malonarian values.

Starpower (Simulation Training Systems). Participants form groups with different economic statuses and seek to improve their own status by learning to trade with each other. However, the most economically viable group is allowed to alter the rules. Alliances form quickly and ingroup-outgroup dynamics become evident, as do assumptions about the uses and abuses of power.

SOURCES FOR
CROSSCULTURAL SIMULATION GAMES

Books

Fowler, Sandra, and Monica Mumford. *Intercultural Sourcebook, Volume 1.* Yarmouth, Maine: Intercultural Press, 1995.

Fowler, Sandra, and Monica Mumford. *Intercultural Sourcebook, Volume 2.* Yarmouth, Maine: Intercultural Press, 1999.

Companies

HRD Press (in association with Workshops by Thiagi)
22 Amherst Road
Amherst, MA 01002
(800) 822-2801
www.hrdpress.com

Intercultural Press
P.O. Box 700
Yarmouth, ME 04096
(800) 370-2665
www.interculturalpress.com

Meridian International Center
1630 Crescent Place NW
Washington, D.C. 20009
(202) 667-6800
www.meridian.org

Moorehead Kennedy Institute
45 John Street, Suite 909
New York, NY 10038
(212) 964-4622

Simulation Training Systems
P.O. Box 910
Del Mar, CA 92014
(800) 942-2900
www.stsintl.com

Workshops by Thiagi
4423 E. Trailridge Road
Bloomington, IN 47408-9633
(812) 332-1478
www.thiagi.com

Websites

AD2000 and Beyond
<www.ad2000.org>

Caleb Project
<www.calebproject.org>

Central Intelligence Agency, World Fact Book
<www.odci.gov/cia/publications/factbook/index.html>

Mission Training International
<www.mti.org/resource.htm>

Oxford Center for Mission Studies
<www.ocms.ac.uk/ms>

Presbyterian Frontier Fellowship
<www.pff.net/links.htm>

Travlang
<www.travlang.com>

United Nations
<www.un.org>

United States Agency for International Development
<www.usaid.gov>

LANGUAGE ACQUISITION PHRASES AND CULTURE/AREA RESEARCH QUESTIONS

LANGUAGE ACQUISITION PHRASES

Being able to extend basic greetings in another language is a wonderful bridge-builder, a basic courtesy. It also can be essential simply to make your way. Memorize these basic phrases in your host language. A good source of online translation for seventy-two languages is Travlang (see appendix two). You can also seek assistance from an international student and from people in the church or ethnic family you visit.

1. Hello/good morning/good afternoon/good evening
2. Sir, madam, teacher, pastor, brother, sister, friend (as appropriate)
3. Goodbye/good night
4. Yes/no/please/thank you
5. You're welcome/pardon me
6. My name is/what is your name
7. How old are you (obviously, you only use this with children)
8. I live in America
9. How do you say/What is that
10. I am a Christian/I love Jesus
11. Praise the Lord/May God bless you
12. How much does this cost
13. Would you sing me a song
14. Where is/where are/here is/here are (your house/the bathroom/the church/the ball)

15. I bring you greetings in the name of Jesus from Christians in America

16. Shall we pray together*

CULTURE RESEARCH QUESTIONS

Use the following questions to guide your research of the region, culture and people you will be visiting. You can find answers through conversations with people from where you will be visiting, through research in the library and through current news reports. (For the complete list of cultural research questions, see Miriam Adeney, *A Time for Risking* [Vancouver, B.C.: Regent College Publishing, 1987], pp. 177-82.)

Geography. Be able to draw a map of the area, noting major cities.

Climate. Determine what the climate will be like while you are there and what kind of clothing is appropriate.

History. Understand a brief overview of the history and contemporary life of the country or people group.

- Government—current political leaders and issues

- Colonial history (if applicable)

- Economy—sources of income, economic issues

- Religious groups—history, other religions and strength of the Christian faith

- Attitude toward the United States

- Major conflicts and current social issues

- Family and social structure

- What is the role of family members?

- What is the normal relationship between husband and wife?

- How much freedom and authority do women and children have?

- What level of formal education would be normal?

- What are appropriate forms of public attire for women and children?

- How do people greet one another?

---

*These recommended phrases are from Miriam Adeney's unpublished manuscript "First Steps in Language Learning."

- To what extent are physical touch and eye contact appropriate? Between whom? When?

Economy.

- What is the normal daily diet?

- How prevalent is poverty?

- How do most people among the group with whom you'll be working earn an income?

- What kind of lifestyle and expenditures do people enjoy?

- What is the dominant form of entertainment?

Religion.

- What are the primary Christian as well as non-Christian groups?

- What is the appeal of the gospel?

- Who are the accepted religious leaders? What kind of training do they receive? How respected are they in the general public?

BOOKMARK AND JOURNAL INSERT

This appendix accompanies chapters seven and eight. To create the bookmark, copy the model onto bright paper and fold it in half so that the prayer of the Missionaries of Charity is on one side of the bookmark and Galatians 2:19-20 on the other. You might want to have it laminated for durability. Use the quotes for prayer and meditation. You may want to keep the bookmark in the Bible for your trip.

The "Twelve Insights" and "Eight Great Questions" should also be printed and laminated—one on each side—so that people can insert them into their journals.

A DAILY PRAYER OF THE MISSIONARIES OF CHARITY IN CALCUTTA

"Dearest Lord, . . .

though you hide yourself

behind the unattractive

disguise of the irritable,

the exacting, and the

unreasonable, may I still

recognize you and say,

'Jesus, . . . how sweet

it is to serve you.' "

GALATIANS 2:19-20

"I have been crucified

with Christ; and it is

no longer I who live,

but it is Christ

who lives in me.

And the life I now live

in the flesh

I live by faith in

the Son of God,

who loved me

and gave himself

for me."

TWELVE INSIGHTS

1   It is not the church of God that has a mission in the world, but the God of mission who has a church in the world.

2   That which is yet to be done in the world is far less than that which has already been done!

3   People are more alike than their cultures.

4   Love is the universal language.

5   Short-term mission is a treasure hunt.

6   In crosscultural encounters we are meeting long-lost, distant relatives.

7   God goes before you—you are catching up on a conversation that God has already begun.

8   God does not send us to be critics.

9   In the treasure hunt of grace, our encouragement and affirmation of people may be our most significant ministry.

10   Our privilege is to lift Jesus up in deed and word.

11   The quality of our love as a team and our incorporation of new team members may be our greatest witness.

12   God will not call us to do something without also giving us the resources to do it.

Taken from *Short-Term Missions Workbook* by Tim Dearborn © 2003 and used by permission of InterVarsity Press, Downers Grove, Illinois 60515.

EIGHT GREAT QUESTIONS

1 *Who am I?*

What can I learn about myself?

2 *Who is God?*

How can my understanding of God grow?

3 *Who are we?*

What can I learn about community and the church?

4 *What is the impact of culture on faith?*

How can I see life and the gospel differently because of what I've experienced?

5 *What's wrong with the world?*

What can I learn about justice, poverty and the causes of suffering?

6 *What does it mean to be a follower of Christ?*

What can I learn about discipleship?

7 *What's of value?*

What can I learn about my lifestyle?

8 *Where am I going?*

What might God call me to be and to do as a result of this experience? What can I learn about my vocation?